BORN IN 1964

HOW TIMES HAVE

CHANGED

WILLIAM DEAN & ELIZABETH ABSALOM

D'AZUR PUBLISHING

BORN IN 1964 HOW TIMES HAVE CHANGED

Published by D'Azur Publishing 2023
D'Azur Publishing is a Division of D'Azur Limited

Copyright © William Dean & Elizabeth Absalom 2023

Elizabeth Absalom & William Dean have asserted their rights under the Copyright, Design and Patents Act 1988 to be identified as the authors of this work.

The language, phrases and terminology within this book are as written at the time of the news reports during the year covered and convey the sentiments at that time. The news reports are taken from internationally recognised major newspapers and other sources of the year in question.
The language does not represent any personal view of the author or publisher.
All Rights Reserved. No part of this publication may be reproduced, stored or transmitted in any form or by any means, electronic, mechanical, digital or otherwise, except under the terms of the Copyright, Designs and Patents Act 1988 or under terms of a licence issued by the publisher. This book is sold subject to the condition that it shall not, by way of trade or otherwise, be lent, resold or hired out, or otherwise circulated without the publishers prior consent in any form or binding or cover other than that in which it is published and without a similar condition, including this condition, being imposed on the subsequent purchaser.
All requests to the Publisher for permission should be addressed to info@d-azur.com.

First published in Great Britain in 2023 by D'Azur Limited
Contact: info@d-azur.com   Visit www.yearbooks.d-azur.com
ISBN 9798865018032

ACKNOWLEDGEMENTS
The publisher wishes to acknowledge the following people and sources:

British Newspaper Archive; The Times Archive; Front Cover Malcolm Watson; p5 Geoff Charles - CND rally, Aberystwyth; DWSav; p7 McKlein & BMW; p9 Omroepvereniging VARA; p11 Jurassica02; p15 Anthony Conti; Doug Coldwell; Ben Tullis; p17 Malcolm Asquith; Terry Whalebone; p19 Fotograaf Onbekend / Anefo; p21 Malcolm Watson; p23 VinciosC; p25 Ecirphr - Own work; p29 Diliff - Own work; ; p30 Victor Hugo King; p31 NASA; p36 eBat; 49 Quatro Valvole; p50 MacDonalds; p58 Vintage Dancer; p64 Science Museum; p64 JodyKingzett; p65 NASA; P65 Salvatore Barbera; p69 Eduard Marmet airliners.net; p71 Wadhurst History Society; p86 Atreyu own work; p86 David Merrett; p87 YouTube; p89 Cédric Janodet; p89 Ken Fielding; p95 Juan Solis; p101 Ethical Trekkin; p101 davidoffnorthide; p105 Corporate Finance Institute; p107 Kingkongphoto; p112 This file is licensed under the Creative Commons Attribution 2.5 Generic license; p115 The Step Blog; p119 Klaviyo; p119 Freshexchange.com; p120 Netflix; p121 Alex Needham ; p121 Willie Duggan; p123 Dan Heap ; p123 Sergeant Rupert Frere; p124 Dave Comeau; p125 John Douglas; p128 Hair and makeup Artists Handbook; Rare Historical Photos; p130 Hagerty.co.uk; PistonHeads; Theteslachannel.com; p131 wish.com; ebaumsworld.com; p132 BMJ; Gillings School of Global Public Health; p133 Nike; p119 McDonalds; Office for National Statistics; Burger King; p140 The Furniture Market; p141 Fatsoma;

Whilst we have made every effort to contact copyright holders, should we have made any omission, please contact us so that we can make the appropriate acknowledgement.

CONTENTS

Life in 1964	p4 - 7
January to December 1964 Weekly News	p8 - 29
Major News Stories of the 1960s	p30 - 31
Life in the 1960s	p32 - 49
Major News Stories of the 1970s	p50 - 51
Life in the 1970s	p52 - 69
Major News Stories of the 1980s	p70 - 71
Life in the 1980s	p72 - 89
Major News Stories of the 1990s	p90 - 91
Life in the 1990s	p92 - 111
Major News Stories of the 21st Century	p112 - 115
Life in the 21st Century	p116 - 127
How Attitudes Have Changed	p128 - 141
The 1964 Calendar	p142

LIFE

Monarch: Queen Elizabeth II
Prime Ministers: Alec Douglas Home (Conservative) (until 16 October). Harold Wilson (Labour)

1964 began under the 13th year of Conservative rule. Alec Douglas-Home presided over a country engulfed in Beatlemania; mini skirts were on the rise; Mods and Rockers took to fighting at the seaside and it was the year The Great Train Robbers were jailed. In October, thirteen years of Tory rule ended when Harold Wilson was elected Labour Prime Minister in the hope of improving poor industrial relations, with a growing number of days lost to strike action and the militant trade unions.

In America, anti-Vietnam war protests were increasing and The Civil Rights Act was made law by President Johnson. The Forth Road Bridge opened; Winston Churchill retired and Radio Caroline, the 'pirate radio station' began broadcasting from a ship just outside UK territorial waters off Suffolk. Elizabeth Taylor married Richard Burton for the first time; BBC aired the first 'Top of the Pops' and BBC 2 took to the air.

Mods (top) and the Forth road bridge (bottom)

FAMOUS PEOPLE WHO WERE BORN IN 1964

12th Jan: Jeff Bezos, Internet entrepreneur
7th Feb: Ray Mears, Woodsman & TV presenter
16th Feb: Christopher Eccleston, British actor
3rd Apr: Nigel Farage, British politician
7th Apr: Russel Crowe, New Zealand born actor
19th Jun: Boris Johnson, British PM
21st Jul: Ross Kemp, British actor
10th Oct: Sarah Lancashire, British actress
21st Nov: Sean Foley, Director, writer, comedian

FAMOUS PEOPLE WHO DIED IN 1964

29th Jan: Alan Ladd, American actor
20th Mar: Brendan Behan, Irish poet & writer
2nd May: Nancy Astor, American born politician
31st Jul: Jim Reeves, American country singer
12th Aug: Ian Fleming, British author
28th Sep: Harpo Marx, American comedian
15th Oct: Cole Porter, American composer
5th Nov: Mabel Lucie Attwell, British illustrator
9th Dec: Edith Sitwell, British poet

In 1964

Born in 1964, you were one of 53.9 million people living in Britain and your life expectancy *then* was 71.2 years. You were one of the 18 births per 1,000 population and you had a 2.1% chance of dying as an infant, a rapidly declining chance as this figure in 1950 was almost 31%.

You were at the beginning of an exciting era of individualism, young people had found their voice and were heard. It was the early days of the feminist movement and saw the growth in campaigns against nuclear weapons and the war in Vietnam and, human rights - whilst we were making great strides towards space travel.

In 1946, an Italian baker, Pietro Ferrero, in Alba, an Italian town known for growing hazelnuts, produced a batch of *Pasta Gianduja*.

This paste, a blend of chocolate with 30% hazelnut paste came originally from Turin during Napoleon's regency, eaten as a block or filling for chocolates. Ferrero made a creamy version and in 1964, his son Michele, revamped *Supercrema gianduja* and renamed it Nutella – an instant success.

In 1964, the standard rate of income tax was 7s 9d in the pound (39%). 'Brut' was launched by the American firm Fabergé Inc. and Pop Tarts were first introduced by Kellogg's.

How Much Did It Cost?

The Average Pay:	£915
The Average House:	£3,092
Loaf of White Bread:	1s 2½d (6p)
Pint of Milk:	9d (4p)
Pint of Beer:	2s 3d (11p)
12mnths Road Tax	£15
Gallon of Petrol:	5s 1d (6p/litre)
Newspapers:	5d - 1s (2-5p)
To post a letter in UK:	3d (1p)
TV Licence	£5 Black & White

Most teenagers owned a transistor radio and listened to pirate Radio Caroline, broadcast from the ship anchored off Felixstowe. On TV we were introduced to the Likely Lads and Playschool was launched for the little ones.

January 1964

IN THE NEWS

WEEK 1 — **"An Added Bonus"** In elation, workers carried their boss home from a factory after receiving surprise bonuses worth over £250,000. In a further revelation, the income tax for the bonuses had been paid by the millionaire Mr Joe Bamford, whose company is worth over £10 million.

WEEK 2 — **"Double the Power"** By 1970, the UK's power output will have doubled, with the implementation of 32 new power stations across the country, costing approximately £400 million a year. The plans come following the ever-increasing demand for electricity in Britain, with the figure also expected to double by then.

"Nuclear Crash" During an intense snowstorm over the skies of Maryland, an American bomber carrying a crew of five and two unarmed nuclear weapons crashed with no fatalities. American authorities confirmed that there was no risk of explosion due to the unarmed nature of the weapons.

WEEK 3 — **"Going Cheap"** Following the government's plans to make resale price maintenance of products including cigarettes, whisky and chocolate illegal, many supermarkets have immediately dropped prices to avoid penalties.

"A Penny a Day" The British Pharmaceutical Industry has revealed that contrary to claims of critics, the taxpayer pays the equivalent of one penny per day per person to fund the NHS. This is in comparison with 3d (1p) on smoking, and 2d on drinking.

WEEK 4 — **"Gorilla Escape"** Two gorillas, who escaped their private zoo at the home of a wealthy landowner in Canterbury, have been recaptured after five hours of freedom roaming the estate; they were guided back to their enclosure using water jets and sticks.

HERE IN BRITAIN

"Heart Over Brawn"

Over 50 removal men have gone back to school for a series of lectures by the Institute of the Warehouse and Removal Industry on how to ease the moving process woes of housewives watching their treasured possessions being uprooted.

With England becoming ever more footloose, the institute feels the need to increase the effectiveness of its workers, by training the typically large strong men, in the ways of gentle social interaction and sensitivity when it comes to the movers' property by stressing the importance of building trust in the first ten minutes.

AROUND THE WORLD

"Twin Towers"

The US government has unveiled plans to erect two 1,350-foot-high skyscrapers in New York City to be the home of the World Trade Centre.

The buildings, set to be complete in 1970, will dominate the Manhattan skyline and assume the title of world's tallest building(s), taking over from the Empire State Building. The 110-story building will cost just shy of $350 million and will contain a mixture of offices, exhibition halls, shops, restaurants and a 250-room hotel. The car park will be able to accommodate 1,600 vehicles at once.

The Monte Carlo Rally

Having completed the last five stages of the Monte Carlo Rally, made up of over 3,000 corners, for the first time ever, a Mini Cooper S has crossed the finish line to win the 1964 rally. Driven by Irishman Patrick 'Paddy' Hopkirk and his co-driver Henry Liddon the little Mini cruised to victory in the face of adversity, racing against almost 300 far more powerful cars on the gruelling circuit.

The British-built, front wheel drive Mini Cooper S cars, proved to be nimble and effective at dealing with the more driver-focused stages, and the new implementation of over 30 different choices of studded tyre proved to suit the little chassis. The cars were fitted with special heated windscreens, an innovation putting them at a significant advantage over the competition. A thin layer of gold is sandwiched by two layers of glass, and small metal strips run horizontally across the screen, which are in turn connected to an electrical system providing heat and preventing the windscreen from icing up.

Conditions this year are the worst they have been for over a decade, with Graham Hill commenting on how the temperatures were so low *'that the ink in my ballpoint pen froze';* he and his co-driver Ian Walker were amongst the large number of drivers not to make the final checkpoint, merely two thirds of the original starting grid making it through to the final stage. The Russians however, failed the previous rounds not through lack of skill or car trouble, but through their inability to speak the French language, with road signs and signposts being incomprehensible to most of the co-drivers. It appeared that the Russians were ill-equipped, with maps only as far as Holland and a severe lack of detail in French road maps.

February 1964

In the News

WEEK 1 — **"Bulls Eye on the Moon"** After a three-day voyage, the US space craft Ranger 6 has hit the moon with minute precision on its intended target but failed to deliver the intended photographs.

WEEK 2 — **"Amphibious Cars"** Britain has placed an order for 50 amphibious cars from West Germany. These can not only act as transport on road and on water but can also link together to form a bridge or ferry.

"Australian Naval Collision" At least 103 people have died following the sinking of the Australian destroyer 'Voyager' which collided with the aircraft carrier 'Melbourne' off the coast of New South Wales.

WEEK 3 — **"M6 Joint Traffic Command"** Three counties' police forces have joined together to patrol the M6 motorway. A manned helicopter will also maintain a permanent patrol of the carriageways.

"6 Mile Taxi Fares to go" The Government has conceded that the current limit for London taxis is too low, and it is likely to be raised to 10 miles. Since the days of horse-drawn cabs no driver has been compelled to take a passenger more than six miles 'on the clock'. Beyond that distance he may bargain with the hirer about the fare.

WEEK 4 — **"The New £10 Note"** After a 19 years absence, the £10 note will return to our currency, bearing a portrait of the Queens head. It ceased to be legal tender in 1945.

"Electric Revolution" A brand new, four seat, electric car, capable of speeds up to 35 mph and to drive 50 miles for 1s 6d (7p), is to make its debut. Recharging takes 10 hours.

Here in Britain

"Too Tall"

The plans for a Mosque in Regents Park have run into complications following the revelation that the building would contravene a five-year-old stipulation that no high building should be erected at the edge of Regents Park.

The land for the Mosque was gifted to the Central London Mosque Trust by George VI in 1944, but it was only last January that the plans for the building were released. Alternative sites are being considered, along with possible alterations to the original designs to accommodate the surroundings.

Around the World

"Kafka in Moscow"

For the first time since the Russian Revolution in 1917, the writings of banned Western authors have been permitted to be published in the country again.

In response to international claims that Russia was adopting a 'cultural isolationism', writers banned under Stalin, and including Franz Kafka, Proust and Joyce, have been published, with a typical communist spin; Kafka is claimed to have been a *'pessimistic victim of the Capitalist environment'*. It is thought that the younger Russian generation is completely ignorant of these classical writers.

THE BEATLES ARE HARMLESS

The Beatles arriving in New York (main) and on a TV show (inset)

"Beatle Bedded by a Bug" was one headline run by an American newspaper amidst the 'Beatlemania' sweeping across the United States at the outset of the band's first USA tour. George Harrison made the front page after catching a minor cold and having to take to his bed ahead of an evening performance. All across New York, teenagers can be seen wearing mop-headed wigs, not having time to grow their own hair to a suitable length. Thousands flocked to the airport to see the band arrive from England.

Many have called the band, *'the most profitable British export of the time'*, with sell out concerts planned all through their tour. Nevertheless, even with their newfound American fame, there was a large degree of hotel confusion upon arriving in New York. The hotel management claims to have not been aware of the coming stars, and instead assumed they were mere British businessmen! People have since been requested to remove their wigs before entering the hotel dining room, and the poor hotel lounge musician has been forced to decline requests for Beatle's songs in the lobby due to them being *'not suitable for the violin'*. However, the fears of an uncontrollable American teenage craze were put to bed after the band's first television performance, watched by thousands of the American public. *'The Beatles are Harmless'* read one American newspaper headline, after the modest and agreeable performance by the band relieved much of the United States population, who have been outraged at the overt sexuality of performers like Elvis.

According to some reports, given the current tensions between England and the US over the British sale of buses to Cuba, the Beatles touring America may help to patch much of the animosity between our countries.

MARCH 1964

IN THE NEWS

WEEK 1 **"Fishy Business"** Fourteen of the sixteen countries in attendance at The European Fisheries Conference have agreed on a new six-mile limit for fishing off a country's coast and a further six mile 'belt' for exclusive fishing rights.

WEEK 2 **"Olympic Grant"** The Minister with a special responsibility for sport, announced a state grant would be made available for the athletes competing in the British Olympic Team at the Tokyo Games next October.

"It's a Boy" It was announced today that the Queen has safely given birth to her fourth child and third son. Both mother and baby are happy and healthy. The boy will be third in line to the throne, ahead of Princess Anne.

WEEK 3 **"Ruby to Death"** Jack Ruby has been sentenced to death having been found guilty of the murder of Lee Harvey Oswald, the alleged assassin of President John F Kennedy.

"Britain's Better Missile" The Polaris Missiles commissioned by the Royal Navy to be housed in its new fleet of submarines, will have a 60% longer range, but be no larger than the ones currently used by the US Armed Forces.

WEEK 4 **"Clacton Rowdyism"** Over 97 young, people have been arrested by Clacton police after disturbances and fights emerged in the town and on the seafront over the weekend.

"Great Train Robbery" After considering their verdicts in secret for 65 hours, the jury for the 'great train robbery' trial found seven men guilty of the theft of over £2 million, and a further nine on charges of conspiracy.

HERE IN BRITAIN

"To the Stocks"

The MP for Middleton and Prestwich has requested that the 1625 Sunday Observance Act be repealed, after members of a bowling club were threatened with *'three hours in the stocks'*.

Police were called to the club the day before one of the groups' fortnightly Sunday handicaps, where they warned the members that if the game went ahead, a three-shilling fine or three hours in the stocks would be the punishment. The ancient law prohibits *'meetings of people outside their own parish on the Lord's Day for any sport or pastime whatsoever'*.

AROUND THE WORLD

"No Daffodil on the Coin"

In Canada, patriotic fervour has been aroused by the omission of the daffodil from the design of the newly minted silver dollar which commemorates the visit of the Fathers of Confederation to Charlottetown and Quebec City in 1864.

The coin contains the French fleurs-de-lys, the English rose, the Scottish thistle and the Irish Shamrock, but a reference to Wales is conspicuously absent. If no daffodil is added to a second minting, Mr Pearson, the PM is unlikely to find 'a welcome in the valley' next time he visits Harlech!

GREAT ST BERNARD TUNNEL

The entrance to the tunnel (inset) which is the only road open in winter between the Aosta valley in Italy and France. The snow covered Grand St Bernard Pass (main picture) is closed October to June

The first ever road tunnel under the Alps was opened in majestic fashion with flags and a ceremony, as five British cars became the first motor vehicles to drive the passage. Having been flown to Geneva, the cars were driven through treacherous conditions and heavy snowfall, reaching speeds of up to 90mph, with a Swiss police escort, in order to reach the tunnel by the scheduled opening time of 8am. The cars triumphantly made it, and it was reported that the only disappointment was the lack of Swiss girls in national costume who were meant to draw lots to see which of the cars would go through the tunnel first. It was rumoured that the conditions got too much for them, so they instead returned home.

Britain was chosen as a suitable host country for the first motor vehicles to pass through because of our great tourist potential, thus a Hillman Imp led a Triumph 2000, a Ford Zephyr, and a Sunbeam Alpine through the tunnel and onto the Mediterranean coast, where they met a contingent of Italian Fiats who were doing the journey in reverse. The aim of the trip was to prove that the journey between London and Genoa could now be done by car in less than 12 hours.

The St Bernard Tunnel is 3.6 miles long, and the roads either side are protected by nine miles of covered galleries to ensure dry and safe roads at all times of year. The name of the tunnel comes directly from the Grand St. Bernard Pass and indirectly from the saint who in AD 1049 founded the hospice high above the tunnel at the summit of the pass. In days gone by, the monks of the hospice used their large St. Bernard dogs to help rescue stranded travellers.

April 1964

IN THE NEWS

WEEK 1 — **"Washington to London"** TWA, one of the premier American airlines, is to introduce a non-stop, seven-hour flight from Washington DC to London and will increase the daily number of flights to Britain from two to three.

"Seat Belt Success" Information from over 800 crashes show that wearing a seat belt reduces risk in the event of an accident by as much as 80%. At present, between 12% and 16% of cars on British roads have them fitted.

WEEK 2 — **"Channel Tunnel Reality"** Now that approval has been given for the project, the Government are being quick to approve the first stages of the planned Channel Tunnel between England and France.

WEEK 3 — **"The Great Escape"** Two German youths have escaped to the west in a light aircraft. Neither of them had any prior piloting experience, but they were undetected by East German police, and landed in a cornfield near Minden.

"Colour TV" Britain should have a full colour TV service no later than 1967, with the final decision on the technical format expected to be made in April 1965.

WEEK 4 — **"Is it Gold?"** There was a major security presence at London Airport when a Russian TU-104 airliner touched down from Moscow carrying a cargo described as 'nine tons of metal', believed to be gold worth nearly £4m.

"Neither Drunk nor Disorderly" Recent figures show a substantial decrease in drunkenness and alcohol consumption amongst young people in recent years. This is supported by lower crime rates, especially in Central London and the Midlands.

HERE IN BRITAIN

"The Little Perishers"

Lord Kilbrandon is amongst many who think that the current Juvenile Court system is too informal and that it is not setting children up for the severity of the law as an adult.

Instead, people like Kilbrandon are more in favour of *'frightening the living daylights out of them'* by using the more formal channels. His view is there is much to be said for delivering the juvenile *'little perisher'* to an *'ugly, uniformed, Superintendent'* at an *'ugly police station'* rather than the *'mollycoddling and reassuring environment of the juvenile court'*.

AROUND THE WORLD

"The Perisher Valley"

Work is in the closing stages for the building of the highest church in Australia, in the rapidly expanding Perisher Valley, New South Wales. The team is working tirelessly to complete the construction before the onslaught of the Australian winter, which would prohibit them from working for the next few months.

The Perisher Valley has undergone an impressive level of growth in recent years, going from a remote settlement with only nine small lodges just five years ago, to a bustling ski resort today, with two hotels, 50 private lodges and 13 ski-lifts.

DARTMOOR DODGERS

Dartmoor Prison Is High Up On Dartmoor At An Altitude Of 420m (1400ft)

Twenty-seven prisoners have sampled the attraction of freedom found when escaping from Dartmoor prison this year. They have escaped by walking away from a working party to overpowering the driver of a fuel tanker delivering to the prison. But one memorable escape was in 1962.

Albert King wriggled and twisted his way out of the jail and left behind one of the biggest escape puzzles in the prison's history. King, who was serving a twelve-year sentence for safe breaking, dug a hole in the floor of his cell and tunnelled a way to a ventilating shaft leading out to the prison yard. He put a dummy in his bed to fool prison officers making the regular night check.

Then, in his pants and vest and with his body apparently greased, he wriggled through the shaft. The next stage was to squeeze through a 14in by 10in grille into the yard. He emerged in the darkness of early morning.

The next barrier was the 20ft high outer wall of the jail. Once over that, it is believed that he was picked up by a friend with clothes and a car. King's getaway was in the pattern of escape which is regarded as a Dartmoor "classic" – that of "Rubber -bones Webb" in 1951 who also dug up his cell floor, left a dummy and wriggled out through a ventilation shaft.

Like Webb, "Corkscrew" King left the jail authorities with some puzzling problems, especially,
• How did he break open the stone floor of his cell without being seen or heard and how did he get rid of the rubble?
• How did he grease his body for the twist through the shaft?
• How did he climb the 20ft high wall? With a ladder like "Rubber Bones Webb"?

May 1964

IN THE NEWS

WEEK 1 — **"Time to Go"** The Times Newspaper office in Moscow has been forced to close, and its Russian correspondent has been expelled from the country, following the Soviet government's belief that the newspaper was *'intentionally slandering the Soviet Union'*.

WEEK 2 — **"1-2 on the Streets of Monaco"** In a double team victory, BRM's 1962 Formula One World Champion Graham Hill came home to win the Monaco Grand Prix, with his teammate, American, R. Ginther, in second place.

"North Sea Oil" The Minister of Power is to allow the issue of licenses to oil companies wishing to explore for natural gas and oil in the British controlled North Sea. 20 applicants are expected, only three of whom are British.

WEEK 3 — **"Revolutionary Hospital"** The Minister of Health has announced plans to replace the run-down St Alfege's Hospital in Greenwich with a new, state of the art, prefabricated one. The new hospital will have 800 beds and cost between £5.5 and £6 million.

"Guilty but Insane" The House of Lords has deemed the courts verdict of 'guilty but insane' to be no more of a verdict than an acquittal and have suggested a 'not guilty by reason of insanity' would make more sense. The old verdict dates to the Trial of Lunatics in 1883.

WEEK 4 — **"Eyesight Requirement"** To accommodate the smaller font of the new seven symbol number plate, eyesight requirements to obtain a driving license are changing. Road users now must read the number plate from 67ft. away rather than 75ft.

HERE IN BRITAIN

"The Weather Master"

A South African has become an entrant to the Warwickshire County Cricket Club's £500 competition to find *'an effective wicket cover'* by claiming an ability to control the weather. The entrepreneur has expressed his desire to come to England and show off his weather changing capability, after claiming success in America, Canada and Europe.

British weather will be *'easy to master'* according to the South African, whose company claims to be able to break up clouds above certain areas, eliminating rain, smog and overcast skies. The cricket club has thanked the man for his suggestion.

AROUND THE WORLD

"Instant Igloo"

The Ontario research foundation has developed what has become known as an 'instant igloo', designed to be a great aid to both civilians and military personnel working in very cold climates. The ingenious design is made from a foamy plastic material which becomes a semi-rigid structure once a match is put to it.

The igloo works via an inbuilt heat source which, when set on fire, causes a rapid expansion of the foam into a 3" thick wall. The plan is to make the shelter an essential for the tool kits of all cold weather operators.

NEW YORK WORLD FAIR

President Johnson officially opened the New York World's Fair, with spirits not dampened by the persisting onslaught of rain nor the civil rights protestors, who largely unsuccessfully, attempted to disrupt proceedings by forming roadblocks and staging protests throughout the city. The 'biggest fair ever staged' as it's been called by the event organisers, is expected to receive over 500,000 visitors on the first day alone, and 200 pavilions are set up and ready to greet them.

The title of crème de la crème of exhibits, however, is won by General Motors, who paid over $50 million, the value of roughly 7,000 Cadillacs, for their stand. The vice president of the company has justified the excessive spend on the demonstration by saying that the money was spent *'to get people in a good mood, to get them thinking big',* and in turn one can only assume he hopes that because of it, people will buy more Cadillacs.

The New York World's Fair was held between October and April in both 1964 and 1965 and was a showcase of 20th Century American business and culture. At a time where public consumerism was a policy being encouraged by the US government, the Western world were invited in to see the products of the 'American Dream' and the triumphant success of the Capitalist system. In that sense, the Fair was an opportunity to explore modern advancements in technology, eat and drink traditional American food and bathe in the successes of small American businesses, but for America itself it was far bigger than that. The country invited not only the Western World, but the Soviet Union and its satellite states, thus turning 'expo' into a political statement, triumphantly showing off the US' economic boom, and showcasing Capitalist ideology to all major world powers.

June 1964

IN THE NEWS

WEEK 1 — **"The Bull Ring Centre"** The Duke of Edinburgh has officially opened what has been hailed as the *'most advanced shopping centre in the world'* in central Birmingham. The centre covers 3.8 acres of land and cost around £8 million to build.

WEEK 2 — **"Hovercraft Trial"** An SRN3 hovercraft has been handed over to the Ministry of Defence to undergo trials on its effectiveness as a military vehicle. It will undergo tests in coastal defence, landings and anti-submarine roles.

"Churchill College" The Duke of Edinburgh paid tribute to the wartime Prime Minister at the opening of the Churchill College at Cambridge University. Lady Churchill and a number of Sir Winston's relatives were present at the ceremony.

WEEK 3 — **"US Army Minis"** The United States army are testing left hand drive variations of British Motor Corporation Minis as part of a study to assess how suitable the vehicles would be for the service.

"Free Nelson Mandela" Nelson Mandela is among seven men who have been arrested and sentenced to life in prison by the South African Government. They were found guilty of planning a 'violent' revolution against the countries racial policies.

WEEK 4 — **"Ferrari Win at Le Mans"** Ferrari have made a clean sweep once again, finishing in first, second and third as they cruised to victory for the fifth consecutive year. The British entered Ferrari, driven by F1 World Champion Graham Hill, came home in second place.

"Total Eclipse of the Moon" Even with Britain covered by a blanket of cloud, the moon eclipse was clearly visible in the early hours of Thursday 25th morning.

HERE IN BRITAIN

"M1 Racetrack"

The Ministry of Transport is investigating British car manufacturers, who are claimed to have been testing prototype cars along the M1 Motorway. Top speed, durability and economy are all features which can be tested on the motorway, but many are said to have been testing cars built for the Le Mans 24-hour race, approaching speeds of almost 200mph.

A spokesperson for Sunbeam said that whilst there may have been some 'running in', there was *'certainly nothing of a high-speed nature'*. The Minister is to be asked to impose a limit of 100 mph on motorways.

AROUND THE WORLD

"Sterilising Starlings"

The latest development in the Unites States' war against starlings is a new chemical designed to sterilise the birds during their mating season. There are estimated to be over 500 million in the US, causing in excess of $50 million worth of damage every year to crops.

The birds are not native to America, and were brought over by an avid Shakespeare fan, who wanted the US to experience the birds spoken about in the playwrights' work. In Washington, 100 public buildings are wired to give starlings an electric shock when they alight on any ledges.

ROLLS MEETS ROYCE

Charles Rolls (left) and Henry Royce (right) with the first ever Rolls Royce car.

To celebrate the 60th anniversary of the now legendary Rolls-Royce car brand, a pageant of Rolls Royce and Bentley cars was held at Goodwood motor circuit this week. Over 1,000 cars attended the rally that ran from 9am. Judges began circulating the paddock at around 11am, when men could still be seen feverishly polishing pristine bodywork, cleaning wheels not out of place on a royal coach and scrubbing engine bays clean enough to eat dinner from. The British culture epitomised by the Rolls-Royce brand is not to be understated, and the cars have become one of Britain's most famous exports, acting as an ambassador of class at every corner of the globe.

Mr Charles Rolls first met Mr Henry Royce at a Manchester hotel in 1904. Rolls, the son of a Lord, was an ex-Etonian and held an engineering degree from Cambridge. By contrast, Royce was the son of a flour miller from Peterborough, whose first job was as a scarecrow on a farm. By this point however, both were relatively successful yet minor businessmen, with Rolls owning a small dealership selling French cars in London, and Royce having just built his first vehicle, the Royce 10hp motor car. The chance meeting of the two men forged a partnership that gifted the world with such elegant machines as the Silver Ghost and the Silver Cloud, not to mention aircraft engines powering the likes of Supermarine Spitfires.

The prizes for the pageant were presented by the Duchess of Richmond, whose husband owns the track and the Goodwood Estate. Ironically, because he did not drive a Bentley or a Rolls-Royce on his return to the Estate, the Duke was refused entry three times to his own racing track by an amateur steward! The volunteer was suitably mortified when he was enlightened.

July 1964

IN THE NEWS

WEEK 1 — **"Egg Hardship"** People living on small incomes have suffered following the Egg Marketing Board's decision to withdraw cheaper, second quality, eggs from the market at the beginning of 1964.

WEEK 2 — **"UK's Share of Concorde Soars"** Britain's share of the development costs of the Concorde airliner have soared to over £140 million. This is an increase of more than 100% from two years ago.

"Subscribe and Save" A new subscription service for a worldwide telephone network linking over 200 million numbers has been announced. The system will direct dial into the network and need no more than 15 numbers.

WEEK 3 — **"MP Pay Rise"** The Leader of the Commons has released plans for an increase in MP's pay, by around £3,000 per year. The plans are designed to be generous enough to avoid it becoming an issue in the future.

"One Million Cars" Recent reports state that there are over 1.25 million private cars in London which make over 8 million journeys every day.

"Independent Malta" Maltese independence is the expected outcome of the recently concluded negotiations between the British and Maltese Governments.

WEEK 4 — **"Winston Churchill Retires Aged 89"** *'The greatest member of Parliament of this or any other age.... The oldest among us can recall nothing to compare with his life and the younger ones among you, no matter however long you live, will never see the like again.'*

HERE IN BRITAIN

"Britain's Tallest Building"

The Minister for Public Building and Works was invited up to the top of the Post Office Tower and using an inscribed silver trowel, smoothed out the last of the concrete during the topping-out ceremony on Britain's tallest building.

The Minister was described as looking *'a bit out of practice'* as he gingerly looked over the edge of the building at the 600ft drop down to Tottenham Court Road. The Minister arrived at the top in the same lift used by the contractors, bringing a large crate of beer and a 'skip' of cement.

AROUND THE WORLD

"Kenyan Sorcery"

In a drive to remove sorcery from the country, the Kenyan African National Union has ordered over 200 witch doctors to hand over their potions and renounce their practices. The group, including 27 women, gathered at a public meeting in Baricho, where they confessed to practicing witchcraft and laid their tools at their feet, to be collected by Kenyan authorities.

One man confessed to the murder of over nine people *'by means of bewitchment'* and his promise to never *'practice again'*, gained a large cheer from the crowd of over 3,000 spectators who had gathered.

THE ROYAL TOURNAMENT

1964

ROYAL TOURNAMENT

This year marks the tercentenary of the Royal Marines, whose marching band will be closing the Royal Tournament. Following the compression of the British Armed Forces into one central command under the Ministry of Defence, this year's tournament is somewhat trimmed down. The watchwords for the event, according to Major General Nelson, the coordinator, are to be *'speed and action'*, and not just to avoid the overrunning and somewhat tedious moments of previous years.

The Major General has promised a shorter yet more punchy and exciting spectacle involving all three wings of the British Armed Forces and he was quick to dispel the fears that the combining and compression of the armed forces would lead to a removal of tradition. The highlights expected include the demonstration of free-fall parachuting drops by the Royal Air Force Paratroopers, and the Royal Navy's annual field gun competition, a pivotal element of the display since 1907.

The idea is said to have been born at a meeting of the National Rifle Association in the 1870s and the Tournament began as a series of skill at arms competitions, quickly evolving to include military bands and a variety of acts and displays. The inaugural display was held in 1880 and shooting, tug of war, tent pegging, tilting at the ring, sword v bayonet and lemon cutting were all present at what proved to a financially unsuccessful event. From there however, the show grew exponentially, with subsequent Tournaments attracting large crowds and it eventually relocated from the Agricultural Hall in Islington to Olympia in London, where it has been held ever since, only taking a brief hiatus' during the World Wars. Crowds still flock to see this demonstration honouring the best of the British Armed Forces in a great occasion of patriotism and military excellence.

August 1964

IN THE NEWS

WEEK 1 — **"US Moon Craft on Course"** The course of the United States Ranger VII moon rocket has been successfully altered so that it is heading for the light side, not the dark side, of the moon. The craft will take thousands of up-close pictures of the moon's surface.

WEEK 2 — **"The Death Zone"** A 19-year-old soldier of the east German People's Army escaped under fire from his comrades to the Federal Republic in Bavaria. Zigzagging through the 'death zone' along the frontier, he collapsed exhausted but uninjured. A total of 19,705 persons have escaped from the east to the west since the Berlin wall was built in 1961.

WEEK 3 — **"Berlin Wall Anniversary"** Approaching the third year since the building of the Berlin Wall, the Social Democratic Party in West Berlin has called for an hour's silence to be observed between 8pm and 9pm.

"Petrol Train Blazes" Twelve petrol wagons were overturned and burst into flames after a collision with a light engine outside Didcot station, Berkshire. Two other wagons in the 48-wagon fuel train also caught fire and the blazing mass stretched along the track before fire fighters arrived.

WEEK 4 — **"Olympic Satellite"** The United States has launched a 'Syncom' satellite which, according to experts, should allow all corners of the world to be able to see the broadcast of the Tokyo Olympics later this year.

"Record Drunk" Britain has broken its record of British adult beer consumption. At an average of nine glasses per person, per week, this puts the country fifth in the global rankings of beer consumption.

HERE IN BRITAIN

"The Pushing and the Fearful"

A study of driving habits of British motorists show that most road users fall into one of two categories, either 'competitive', or 'non-competitive'. The 'competitive category' display 'aggressive' and 'pushing' tendencies, *'taking a positive pleasure in overtaking and become completely frustrated when overtaken'.* The 'non-competitive' are more likely to show 'fearful' and 'careful' driving characteristics *'not becoming involved in overtaking and his attitude to being overtaken may be 'good luck to him'.'* Many drivers change from being 'aggressive' in adolescence to 'careful' in middle age'.

AROUND THE WORLD

"Early Marriages"

A Professor at Cornell University has reported that more women in the US marry at the age of 18 than any other age, and that the average age of marriage is dropping rapidly.

The report continues that, assuming all 18-year-old women have a baby, and then go on to have four children in total, the US population would grow at a rate of over 2 million a year. The Professor warns that merely decreasing the average number of children per family is much less important than postponing the age of marriage.

The Great Steam Fair

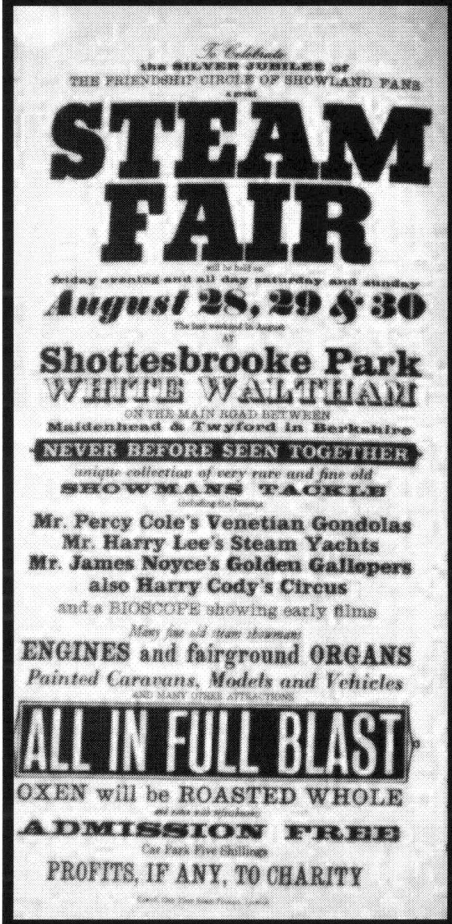

Shottesbrooke Park, in White Waltham, Berkshire was the 100-acre site chosen by Mr John Smith to host a 'Great Steam Fair' to celebrate the silver jubilee of the Friendship Circle of Showland Fans. The fair brought together half a century of fairground rides into one fantastic event. All of the rides and stands were powered by steam engines, ranging from old to modern, and the whole show was designed as *'a nostalgic exhibition, organised for adults, by adults.'* Mr Smith believes that old fairground rides are spectacles that should be enjoyed by the whole family, unlike the modern, fast paced roller coasters that are tailored to teenage adrenaline junkies. The Fair felt like stepping back in time.

The rides themselves, looked as if they had not aged a bit, and instead were as polished as when they were first set up, which was in some cases, over four decades ago. They move slowly enough for the riders to see and enjoy the elaborate paintings and carvings and are a joy to watch. Wherever they go, they attract crowds who just stand and stare. The steam-generated fairground organs, beautiful to look at, grinding out old-time music are very different from today's normal loudspeaker output. These beautifully elegant rides included a horse drawn fire-engine, a Venetian style gondola, and a 'steam yacht' swing, capable of carrying 40 people in each of its two cars and which provided the most fast paced excitement you could expect from the lazy, elegant fair.

The event was so well organised and advertised that it attracted locals, enthusiasts and showfolk alike, all of whom enjoyed a day out as if they had stepped back 30 years. It even drew attention from a company of filmmakers, who have made a documentary recording the event.

September 1964

IN THE NEWS

WEEK 1 — **"Forth Road Bridge"** The Forth Road Bridge has been opened by the Queen. A coastal mist which had concealed it since daylight, partially cleared just before the ceremony

"Jet Noise with Bingo" Bingo will be played at five sites around the Farnborough Show airfield for scientists to record how concentration is affected by aircraft noise.

WEEK 2 — **"Whites Stay Away"** Prince Edward County, Virginia, which closed its public schools five years ago to avoid desegregation, reopened them, but only three of the 1,600 children who attended were white.

"Families Flee" 11 East German children and three adults successfully smuggled themselves across the East German border into West Germany by hiding in a lorry full of pig carcasses.

WEEK 3 — **"London Panda to Moscow"** London Zoo authorities have said that they are willing to send their £12,000 giant panda, Chi-Chi, to Moscow to be mated with the Russian male An-An. Outside China these are the only giant pandas in captivity.

"Continental Shelf Oil" Britain has become the first North Sea country to permit a full-scale search for oil and gas on the sea bed by granting licences to 22 major oil companies.

WEEK 4 — **"Port Galore on A4"** A lorry carrying over 1,400 gallons of port was involved in a crash on the A4. One cask rolled off and port spilt over the road. Five more casks sprang leaks. Passers-by were queuing to collect the drips in milk bottles and jugs.

"Accessible for All" Travel agencies are expecting a sharp increase in bookings of foreign holidays from next year as they revealed a holiday can cost as little as £150.

HERE IN BRITAIN

"Filling the Moat"

Police have been forced to deal with students attempting to fill the moat of the Tower of London with water from the River Thames after they stormed the Tower with buckets to publicise their 'rag week'. They said they were filling the moat to celebrate *'Oliver Cromwell's historic swim in it'*.

Over 130 students and their girlfriends from Farnborough Technical College and the Royal Aircraft Establishment arrived at the Tower on three packed coaches wearing fancy dress. The students claimed that *'victory is ours'* before boarding their coaches and returning home.

AROUND THE WORLD

"Ashes Stay in England"

Although Australia won the Ashes this year, the priceless urn will remain in England and not be flown out to an exhibition in Sydney later this month. Instead, a replica urn will be used to commemorate the Aussie's victory over England in the cricket.

It has been revealed that the Ashes have in fact, never left England due to safety concerns, and remain at Lords Cricket Ground all year round. Other exhibits will however be on display, including the scorecard from the 1882 match, where Australia won for the first time.

HE WHO MAKES THINGS SPROUT

The Aztec rain God, Tlaloc, translated literally as 'he who makes things sprout' has caused controversy and sparked the interest of many Mexican people after it was revealed by the Mexican government that his statue would be moved from his sacred resting place, where he has remained for centuries, to the site of the new National Museum. Many of Tlaloc's supporters and devotees are angry at the statue's removal and have foretold many disasters in the coming months. The people of Coatlinchan, where the statue was moved from, have predicted his moving is the cause of *'torrents of rain and floods'* in the poor areas of Mexico. Many came to watch the statue be taken away, and although having been persuaded to put national pride before local, they watched the god's departure with sullen faces, only brightening when they were placated by offers of new village amenities such as a school and a clinic.

The statue dates back to the early 16th Century, and stands 27 feet tall, weighing 167 tons. It is the tallest statue on the Continent and required a 72 wheeled trailer, pulled by two 600hp tractors and pushed by a 220hp bulldozer to maintain an average speed of just 2 miles per hour. As the cortege entered Mexico City with the god, strapped down *'like Gulliver by the Lilliputians'*, telephone and electric cables had to be cut and later replaced, to allow sufficient headway.

Tlaloc's following began during the time of the Aztec's who inhabited Mexico between the 14th and 16th Centuries. Five months of their 18-month ritual year were dedicated to Tlaloc, children were sacrificed to him on the first and third months and the rain priests ceremonially bathed in the lake during the sixth to obtain rain.

October 1964

IN THE NEWS

WEEK 1 — **"Firebombs in Belfast"** Violence has broken out on a serious scale in Belfast, with crowds taking police days to disperse. Several were injured in violence between police and pro-republican protesters, and two police patrol vehicles were destroyed by firebombs.

WEEK 2 — **"Jet-Powered Three-Wheeler"** The 'fastest man on wheels' title has been retaken by American Craig Breedlove, with a speed of 468 mph in the 'Spirit of America', across the Bonneville salt flats in his three wheeled jet powered car.

"Queen's Reception in Canada" Her Majesty the Queen was welcomed by large crowds in Ottawa, Canada, when she laid a wreath during the ceremony for Thanksgiving Day.

WEEK 3 — **"Labour Victory"** In the closest General Election on record, a near dead heat, Mr Harold Wilson will be the youngest Prime Minister of the century to lead the fifth British Labour Government.

"Trawler Tantrum" The detention of the 'Prince Philip Trawler' for eight days by the Icelandic authorities has caused a protest by the British Trawlers Federation. The ship's Captain claims they were more than a mile outside Iceland's 12-mile radius when captured.

WEEK 4 — **"An Independent Zambia"** Northern Rhodesia, a former British Protectorate, has officially declared independence, along with the assumption of a new name, Zambia. The change marks the end of 73 years of British control.

"New Fastest Man" For the fourth time this year, the title of 'the fastest man on wheels' has changed hands again. American Art Arfos reached 536mph in his bright green jet powered car across the Bonneville salt flats in Utah.

HERE IN BRITAIN

"Tin Openers to Go"

Britain's largest supplier of tins, Metal Box, may have introduced the actual 'best thing since sliced bread' in the new Easy Open Tin, which has a tin opener built in, much like the lid of a fizzy drinks can. A tab fixed to the end of the tin, when pulled, tears a hole in the metal, allowing the lid to be pulled away.

This marks the end of a century-old uneasy marriage between the canner and the tin-opener. In 1830 a hammer and chisel were the tools recommended to the serious opener of tins.

AROUND THE WORLD

"Not Big Enough for Two"

For 15 hours, two women fought a 'tug of war' over the purchase of an English bicycle for sale on special offer, at a discount store in New York. Encouragement and food came from friends and family as neither woman dared to take her hand off the handlebars.

After being removed at closing time, the women returned the following morning, where the manager made them more comfortable with a pair of deck chairs. In the end, the shopkeeper sold the women two identical bicycles at the cut price of $10 (£3 1s 5d).

DONKEYS - VALUE TO VERMIN

Feral donkeys (left) descend from abandoned or escaped pack animals (above)

A six-week drive to kill up to 100,000 wild donkeys which are damaging valuable cattle grazing country in the far north of Western Australia is now well under way. The annual drive, organised by independent shooters and cattle station owners, has gained international recognition in recent years, and shooters from several countries have shown interest despite some animal lovers in Britain expressing concern about the possibility of donkeys being left wounded to die slowly.

The first three donkeys arrived in New South Wales in 1793 but they were not much used by Europeans who continued to use the horse as their main mode of transportation, only coming into wider use with the opening up of Central and Western Australia in the 1860s where they were extensively used until the late 1930s for freight haulage in areas where horse and bullock teams perished. Problems had also arisen when horses began to become sickened by some of the native poisonous plants. When donkeys proved to be resistant to these plants, more donkeys were brought in and when motorised transport took over, the teamsters - the men who drove the teams of donkeys - simply set their donkeys free, as they had no wish to shoot them.

Conditions were ideal for the donkeys to prosper in their feral (a wild animal that once belonged to a primarily domesticated species) state, as they graze all year round on grass, shrubs and tree bark, for 6 to 7 hours a day. This seriously affects the environment and produces many problems including polluting water holes with the potential to make native plants and animals extinct and, most importantly to ranch owners, the donkeys affect local agriculture, by over grazing pastureland, destroying fences and even infecting domestic animals with disease.

November 1964

IN THE NEWS

WEEK 1 — **"200,000 To East Berlin"** As per the new passes, over 200,000 West Germans made the crossing to East Germany to visit family members during the first two days of the programme.

WEEK 2 — **"Margate Pier Fire"** The 80-year-old pavilion at the end of Margate Pier has been badly damaged by fire. The building housed a cafe, bars and amusement slot machines used by thousands of holiday makers in the summer.

"Remembrance Sunday" Whitehall was packed on the crisp sunny morning to observe the Queen place her wreath on the Cenotaph on the National Day of Remembrance.

WEEK 3 — **"Lucky for Some"** The Pope has given away the 'triple crown' he was given by his old archdiocese when he became Pope. The tiara is valued at over £50 million and will go to benefit the poor.

"No British Arms to SA" The export of arms from Britain to South Africa is to be banned by the Government as soon as existing contracts have been fulfilled.

WEEK 4 — **"Football Coupons Seized"** Over 100 football pool coupons have been seized by American customs on their way from Bermuda to London after US officials deemed the coupons to be 'lottery tickets' and thus not legal to pass through the United States.

"£22 For All Mothers" All of Britain's mothers are to receive a £22 government grant, no matter where they have their baby. Previously, women who gave birth at home would receive £22, and those in hospital, £16.

"Woman Customs Commissioner" For the first time ever, a woman has been appointed Commissioner for Customs and Excise.

HERE IN BRITAIN

"Selling Britain"

The Chairman of the Association of British Travel Agents has spoken of the Country's duty to 'sell' Britain to potential tourists. *'Britain's pageantry and traditions had great appeal, but why'* he asked, *'could not a ceremony like Trooping the Colour be staged at Wembley Stadium or the White City, where it could be seen by 10,000 people, instead of Horse Guards Parade where only a fraction of that number – most of them, privileged - could be accommodated? Why not cameras in the House of Commons, for people in the lobby to watch Parliament at work?'*

AROUND THE WORLD

"No Sugar"

Diwali, the happiest of all the festivals of the Hindu calendar, has been celebrated in a shroud of anxiety for the future this year.
It is a time for new beginnings and treats and a time for visiting, and the Hindu housewife who has no sweetmeats or drinks of sweetened milk or tea to offer, will feel she is not honouring Lakshmi, goddess of good fortune and abundance.
But sugar is scarce and to obtain enough just for the family, means long hours in queues or high prices on the black market.

REMEMBER REMEMBER

Guy Fawkes Day celebrations this year were particularly rowdy. By midnight, there were 98 arrests in Trafalgar Square. Seventy-two were accused of throwing fireworks, four of paddling in the fountains, 10 of insulting behaviour, one of obstructing police, four of assault on police, two of obstructing the foot way, three of threatening behaviour, and two of being drunk and disorderly. More than 40 teenagers were arrested after a 'pitched battle' between Mods and Rockers on Hampstead Heath and underground trains were delayed because of gangs of teenagers letting off fireworks. At Margate, police managed to contain a crowd of 800 young people who were watching fireworks on the sea-front, until 300 ran off through the old town, causing chaos and smashing windows.

The nominal excuse for this annual celebration on 5th November, was the unsuccessful attempt by Guy, or Guido, Fawkes and a group of radical English Catholics to assassinate King James I by blowing up the Houses of Parliament. The plot went horribly wrong, and all the conspirators were executed. Catholicism in England had been heavily repressed under the reign of Elizabeth I with many priests put to death and Mass made illegal, so when the protestant James I came to the throne, the Catholic's hopes for change were high.

It soon became clear however that James did not support religious tolerance any more than Elizabeth had done, he condemned Catholicism as a superstition and ordered all Catholic priests to leave England. Hence the 'Gunpowder Plot' was hatched. Fawkes would light a fuse during the opening session of Parliament, James would be blown sky high, and he would escape by boat across the Thames. James's daughter would be kidnapped, installed as a 'puppet queen' and eventually married off to a Catholic thereby restoring the Catholic monarchy.

December 1964

IN THE NEWS

WEEK 1 — **"Tensions Brewing"** Argentina has brought her claim to the British administered Falkland Islands (Islas Malvinas) before the United Nations General Assembly. The Argentinian Foreign Minister claims the British 'illegally' took the island in 1833.

WEEK 2 — **"Steel Lifeboat Success"** After 4,500 miles of sea trials, a steel lifeboat acquired from the US coastguard has proved to be extremely effective, and The Royal National Lifeboat Institution is likely to be commissioning several of its type to be built in Britain.

"Law of Sunday Observance" Religious authorities have supported the relaxation of many previously prohibited activities on a Sunday. These included amateur sports and cinema openings. Professional sport is, however, still restricted.

WEEK 3 — **"Free Prescriptions"** The Minister of Health has announced that the NHS will be returning to free prescriptions in February next year, ending the 2s charge implemented in 1961.

"Drink Driving Clamp Down" 1964 is likely to be the last year when only voluntary measures are placed on drink driving. The Ministry of Transport is taking heed from other European countries who have already implemented legal regulations.

WEEK 4 — **"Queen's Christmas Message"** Her Majesty's traditional message was televised and addressed the important role of the Commonwealth.

"Snowed In" A giant blizzard swept across Britain causing over 3 million TV's to blackout over thirty counties.

HERE IN BRITAIN

"Well Nigh Perfect"

An 80-year-old Edinburgh man pleaded guilty to counterfeiting over 14,000 2-shilling (10p) pieces, born out of his resistance to seeking National Assistance. The money was described as 'well-nigh perfect' and given high praise by the chief assayer at the Royal Mint, who said that specimens sent to him for evaluation, *'are of excellent quality produced by an expert craftsman'.*
The man had been deceiving the banks and shops for over six years and was caught by accident when police were attending another matter in his building. He was sentenced to prison for two years.

AROUND THE WORLD

"Indian Cyclone"

India and Ceylon have been hit by devastating floods and cyclones that have wrecked homes and towns in the South of the country. Over 200 million rupees worth of damage has been reported, with at least 350 people unaccounted for from the cyclone that hit Ceylon. The devastation caused by the disaster has been recorded as the worst in living memory. Over 1,500 bodies have been washed up on newly formed shores and thousands of acres of crops have been destroyed and schools, hospitals and homes flattened. The exact number of dead will never be known.

THE TRAFALGAR TREE

Norway's annual gift of a Christmas tree is in pride of place at Trafalgar Square. The 63-foot, four ton, tree, is one of the most impressive yet, and thousands of people flocked to London on Thursday to watch the Norwegian Ambassador ceremoniously switch the tree lights on. London's Regent Street and Oxford Street Christmas illuminations were switched on last week.

The first tree was sent from Oslo in 1947 as a token of gratitude to the British people for their help during the second world war when Great Britain was Norway's closest ally. London was where the Norwegian King Haakon VII and his government fled as their country was occupied, and it was from here that much of Norway's resistance movement was organised. Both the BBC and its Norwegian counterpart NRK would broadcast in Norwegian from London, something that was both an important source of information and a boost of morale for those who remained in Norway, where people would listen in secret to their forbidden radios. The idea to send a pine to Britain was first conceived by the Norwegian naval commando, Mons Urangsvå, who sent a tree from the island of Hisøy which had been cut down during a raid to London in 1942 as a gift to King Haakon and King George V decided that it should be installed in Trafalgar Square where it stood *'evergreen with defiant hope'*.

The trees come from the snow-covered forest area surrounding Oslo, known as "Oslomarka", an area populated with moose, lynx, roe deer, and even the odd wolf, and legions of pine trees. A worthy tree is located by the head forester and space is cleared around it to allow light from all angles, and it is tended through the years to secure optimal growth.

THE MAJOR NEWS STORIES

1960

May: Princess Margaret marries photographer, Anthony Armstrong-Jones at Westminster Abbey. It is the first royal marriage to be televised.

Nov: "Lady Chatterley's Lover" sells 200,000 copies in one day following its publication since the ban enforced in 1928 is lifted.

1961

Jan: The farthing, used since the 13th Century, ceases to be legal tender in the UK.

Apr: The US attack on "The Bay of Pigs" in Cuba was defeated within two days by Cuban forces under the direct command of their Premier, Fidel Castro.

1962

Jan: An outbreak of smallpox infects 45 and kills 19 in South Wales. 900,000 people in the region are vaccinated against the disease.

Dec: The "Big Freeze" starts in Britain. There are no frost-free nights until 5 March 1963.

1963

June: Kennedy: 'Ich bin ein Berliner' The US President Kennedy, has made a ground-breaking speech in Berlin offering American solidarity to the citizens of West Germany.

Aug: 'The Great Train Robbery' on the travelling Post Office train from Glasgow to Euston, takes place in Buckinghamshire.

1964

Mar: Radio Caroline, the 'pirate radio station' begins regular broadcasting from a ship just outside UK territorial waters off Felixstowe, Suffolk.

Oct: After thirteen years in power, the Conservatives are beaten by Labour at the General Election and Harold Wilson becomes Prime Minister.

The Tiller Girls At The London Palladium

1962: In April, the five-month-old strike by Equity, the actors' union, against the Independent television companies, ends, with actors gaining huge increases in basic pay rates.

1963: John F. Kennedy, the 35th president of the United States, was assassinated on November 22 in Dallas, Texas, while riding in a presidential motorcade. He was with his wife Jacqueline, Texas Governor John Connally, and Connally's wife Nellie when he was fatally shot from a nearby building by Lee Harvey Oswald. Governor Connally was seriously wounded in the attack. The motorcade rushed to the local hospital, where Kennedy was pronounced dead about 30 minutes after the shooting. Mr Connally recovered.

OF THE 1960s

1969 APOLLO 11. Neil Armstrong becomes the first man to walk on the moon. "One small step for man, one giant leap for mankind."

1965: In January, Sir Winston Churchill dies aged 90. Sir Winston served as Prime Minister of the United Kingdom from 1940-45 and again from 1951-1955. He is best known for his wartime leadership as PM.

1965

Mar: 3,500 US Marines, the first American ground combat troops arrive in Da Nang, South Vietnam.

Aug: Elizabeth Lane is appointed as the first ever female High Court Judge. She is assigned to the Family Division.

1966

Jun: The first British credit card, the Barclaycard, is introduced by Barclays. It has a monopoly in the market until the Access Card is introduced in 1972.

Sept: HMS Resolution is launched at Barrow-in-Furness. It is the first of the Polaris ballistic missile submarines, armed with 16 Polaris A missiles.

1967

Jan: Donald Campbell, the racing driver and speedboat racer, was killed on Coniston Water whilst attempting to break his own speed record.

Dec: The Anglo-French Concorde supersonic aircraft was unveiled in Toulouse, France.

1968

Jun: The National Health Service reintroduces prescription charges, abolished by the Labour Govt. in 1965, at 2s 6d.

Sep: The General Post Office divides their single rate postal service into two. First-class letters at 5d and second-class at 4d.

1969

Mar: The Queen opens the Victoria Line on the London Underground. It is the first entirely new Underground line in London for 50 years.

Dec: The abolition of the death penalty for murder, having been suspended since 1965, was made permanent by Parliament.

The Home

At the beginning of the decade, the wireless was still the usual form of entertainment in the home and children could sit comfortably to "Listen with Mother" on the Light Programme and mother could carry on listening to "Woman's Hour" afterwards.

However, television was becoming increasingly affordable, and the two channels, BBC and ITV were joined in 1965 by BBC2. Dr Finlay's Casebook; The Black and White Minstrel Show; Top of the Pops; Perry Mason and Z Cars were the most popular shows of the 60's.

In 1962 the BBC bravely introduced a new satirical show, "That Was the Week That Was" which proved a big hit and by 1969, the BBC was converting programmes to colour.

Children's pocket money, probably 6d (2.5p) a week in the early years, could buy sweets. Black Jacks and Fruit Salads (4 for a penny (0.5p)), sweet cigarettes, lemonade crystals, gob stoppers, flying saucers or toffees, weighed by the shopkeeper in 2oz or 4oz paper bags. All could be eaten whilst reading a copy of The Beano or Dandy, Bunty or Jack and Jill comics.

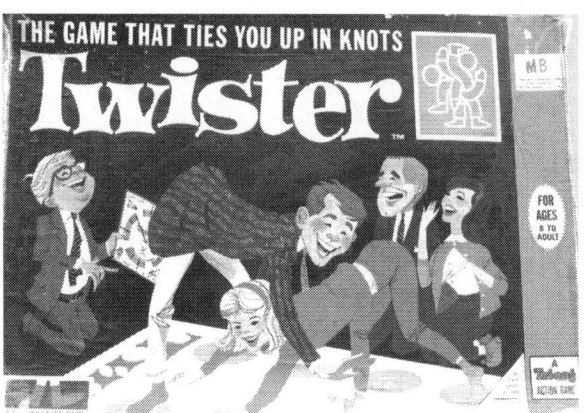

The simple, yet addictive party game Twister was introduced in 1966.

IN THE 1960s

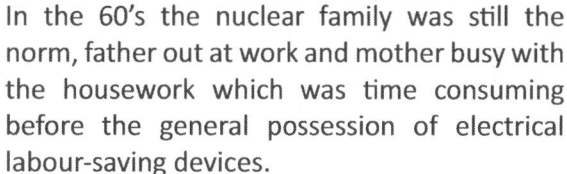

In the 60's the nuclear family was still the norm, father out at work and mother busy with the housework which was time consuming before the general possession of electrical labour-saving devices.

Washing up was done by hand and laundry gradually moved to machines over the decade.

Twin tubs, one for washing and one for Spinning, became popular in the late 60's and were usually wheeled into the kitchen to be attached to the cold tap and afterwards, have the waste-water emptied into the sink. The 'housewife' had to be at home to transfer the wet washing from the washing tub to the spinning tub.

By the end of the 60's, 58% of households had a small refrigerator but no fridge/freezers, so shopping was still done regularly and, typically, meals were home cooked.

Chicken was expensive but beef was cheaper and olive oil came only in tiny bottles from the chemist to help clean your ears!

In Britain, the domestic freezer is still a luxury but by the mid 60's, some 700m fish fingers were among the 60,000 tons of frozen fish consumed with peas from 35,000 acres and 120,000 quick-frozen chickens.

Goods came to you. The milkman delivered the milk to your doorstep, the baker brought the baskets of bread to the door, the greengrocer delivered and the 'pop man' came once a week with 'dandelion and burdock', 'cherryade' or 'cream soda' and the rag and bone man called down the street for your recycling.

33

Art and Culture

1960 - 1963

1960 Frederick Ashton's 'La Fille Mal Gardée' premieres by The Royal Ballet at the Royal Opera House.
In court, Penguin Books who published 'Lady Chatterley's Lover' by DH Lawrence, is found not guilty of obscenity.

1961 The 'Betting & Gaming Act' comes into force which allows the operating of commercial Bingo halls.
'Ken' is introduced in the US as a boyfriend for 'Barbie'.

1962 Margot Fonteyn and Rudolf Nureyev first dance together in a Royal Ballet performance of Giselle, in London.
Dec John Steinbeck, American author is awarded the Nobel Prize in Literature. Aleksandr Solzhenitsyn's novella, "One Day in the Life of Ivan Denisovich" is published in Russia.

1963 The first Leeds Piano Competition is held, and Michael Roll is the winner.
Authors CS Lewis and Aldous Huxley both die on 23 November, but news of their deaths is overshadowed by the assassination of JFK.

Margot Fonteyn and Robert Helpmann performing The Sleeping Beauty.

Their partnership has been described as the greatest of all time.

1964 - 1969

1964 BBC television airs the first 'Top of the Pops'. Dusty Springfield is the very first artist to perform, with 'I Only Want to Be With You'.
Ernest Hemingway's memoirs of his years in Paris, 'A Moveable Feast' is published posthumously by his wife.

1965 Rembrandt's painting 'Titus' is sold at Christie's London fetching the then record price of 760,000 guineas. (£798,000).
The f*** word is spoken for the first time on television by Kenneth Tynan and two weeks later, Mary Whitehouse founds The National Viewers' and Listeners' Association.

1966 'Rosencrantz and Guildenstern Are Dead' by Tom Stoppard has its debut at the Edinburgh Festival Fringe.
BBC1 televises 'Cathy Come Home', a docudrama that is viewed by a quarter of the British public and goes on to influence attitudes to homelessness.

1967 **'The Summer of Love'.** Thousands of young 'flower children' descend on the west coast of America, for hippie music, hallucinogenic drugs, spiritual meditation and free-love.
BBC radio restructures. The Home Service becomes Radio 4, the Third Programme becomes Radio 3 and the Light Programme is split between Radio 1 (to compete with pirate radio) and Radio 2.

1968 The BBC repeat of the twenty-six episodes of 'The Forsyte Saga' on Sunday evening television, leads to reports of 'publicans and vicars complaining it was driving away their customers and worshippers, respectively' and of 'Evensong services being moved to avoid a clash'.

1969 The Beatles perform together for the last time on the rooftop of Apple Records in London. The impromptu concert was broken up by the police.

IN THE 1960s

The three-day Woodstock Music Festival was held in August 1969 on a dairy farm in Bethel, New York. Nearly half a million young people arrived for "An Aquarian Experience: 3 Days of Peace and Music." Now known simply as Woodstock, the festival was a huge success, but it did not go off without a hitch. The almost 500,000 people who turned up was unexpected and caused the organisers a headache which necessitated venue changes and this was before the bad weather, muddy conditions, lack of food and unsanitary conditions made life even more difficult.

Surprisingly, the event passed off peacefully, this fact attributed by most, to the amount of sex, psychedelic drugs and rock 'n roll that took place. Others say, couples were too busy 'making love not war' to cause trouble, either way, Woodstock earned its place in the halls of pop culture history fame.

"American artist Andy Warhol premieres his "Campbell's Soup Cans" exhibit in Los Angeles".

Andy Warhol famously borrowed familiar icons from everyday life and the media, among them celebrity and tabloid news photos, comic strips, and, in this work, the popular canned soup made by the Campbell's Soup Company. When he first exhibited "Campbell's Soup Cans", the images were displayed together on shelves, like products in a grocery aisle. At the time, Campbell's sold 32 soup varieties and each one of Warhol's 32 canvases corresponds to a different flavour, each having a different label. The first flavour, introduced in 1897, was tomato.

Each canvas was hand painted and the fleur de lys pattern round each can's bottom edge was hand stamped. Warhol said, "I used to drink Campbell's Soup. I used to have the same lunch every day, for 20 years, I guess!"

Films

1960 - 1963

1960 **Ben Hur**, the religious epic, was a remake of a 1925 silent film with a similar title and had the largest budget ($15.175m) and the largest sets built of any film produced at the time.

1961 Billy Wilder's risqué tragi-comedy **The Apartment** won the Academy Award for Best Picture. Starring Jack Lemmon and Shirley MacLaine, it tells a story of an ambitious, lonely insurance clerk who lends out his New York apartment to executives for their love affairs.

1962 New Films released this year included, **Lolita** starring James Mason and Sue Lyon. **Dr No**, the first James Bond film, starring Sean Connery and Ursula Andress and **What Ever Happened to Baby Jane?** a horror film with Bette Davis

1963 **Lawrence of Arabia,** based on author TS Eliot's book 'Seven Pillars of Wisdom' and starring Peter O'Toole and Alec Guinness won the Oscar for Best Picture.
The publicity of the affair between the stars, Elizabeth Taylor and Richard Burton, helped make **Cleopatra** a huge box office success but the enormous production costs, caused the film to be a financial disaster.

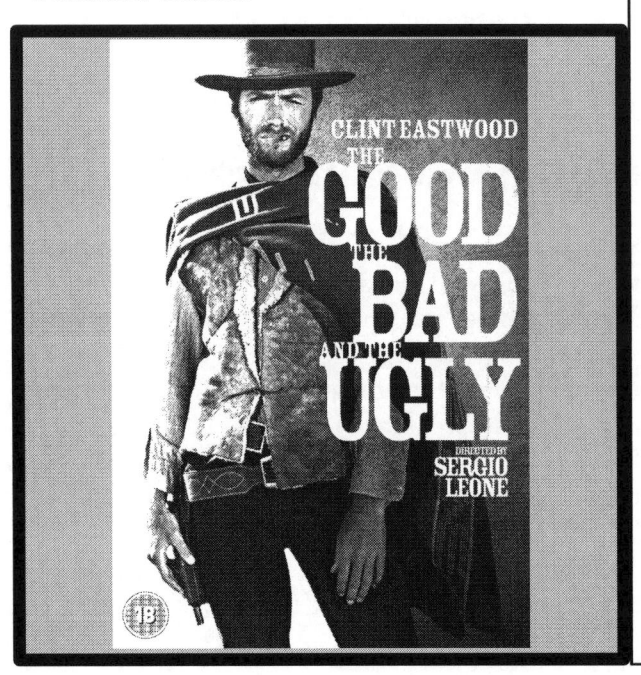

1964 - 1969

1964 The historical adventure, sex comedy romp **Tom Jones** won four Oscars, Best Picture, Best Director, Best Adapted Screenplay and Best Musical Score. Albert Finney starred as the titular hero and Susannah York as the girl he loves.

1965 Winning the Oscar this year, the film **My Fair Lady,** based on George Bernard Shaw's play 'Pygmalion', tells the story of Eliza Doolittle and her quest to 'speak proper' in order to be presentable in Edwardian London's high society. Rex Harrison and Audrey Hepburn starred and it became the 2nd highest grossing film of the year just behind **The Sound of Music** which won the Academy Award the following year.

1966 **The Good, the Bad and the Ugly** was directed by Sergio Leonie, the Italian director who gave rise to the term 'spaghetti western'- a genre of westerns produced and directed by Italians. Clint Eastwood was the Good, Lee Van Cleef, the Bad and Eli Wallach, the Ugly. The film was a huge success and catapulted Clint Eastwood to fame.

1967 The fun filled seduction of Benjamin Braddock by Mrs Robinson in **The Graduate** made the film the biggest grossing production of the year world-wide.

1968 The famous quote "They call me Mister Tibbs" comes from **In the Heat of the Night** where Sidney Poitier plays Virgil Tibbs, a black police detective from Philadelphia, caught up in a murder investigation in racially hostile Mississippi. Rod Steiger is the white chief of police.

1969 **Oliver** the musical based on Dicken's novel and Lionel Bart's stage show, carried off the Oscar for Best Picture.
Editor's Note: The Academy Awards are held in February and each year's awards are presented for films that were first shown during the full preceding calendar year from January 1 to December 31 Los Angelis, California. Source: Wikipedia

IN THE 1960s

THE FIRST JAMES BOND FILM!

HARRY SALTZMAN and ALBERT R. BROCCOLI PRESENT IAN FLEMING'S **DR. NO** TECHNICOLOR — SEAN CONNERY AS 007, URSULA ANDRESS, JOSEPH WISEMAN, JACK LORD. Screenplay by Richard Maibaum, Johanna Harwood, Berkely Mather. Directed by Terence Young. Produced by Harry Saltzman.

This was the first-ever launch of a James Bond film in a cinema and was attended by the stars, Sean Connery and Ursula Andress together with the James Bond creator Ian Fleming. The plot of this British spy film revolves around James Bond who needs to solve the mystery of the strange disappearance of a British agent to Jamaica and finds an underground base belonging to Dr No who is plotting to disrupt the American space launch with a radio beam weapon. The film was condemned by The Vatican as "a dangerous mixture of violence, vulgarity, sadism, and sex".

1962 : "West Side Story" Wins The Academy Awards "Best Picture" category.

The musical with lyrics by Stephen Sondheim and music by Leonard Bernstein was inspired by the story of William Shakespeare's "Romeo and Juliet". Set in the mid 1950s in Upper West Side of New York City, which was then, a cosmopolitan working-class area, it follows the rivalry between the Jets and the Sharks, two teenage street gangs from different ethnic backgrounds.

The Sharks are from Puerto Rico and are taunted by the white Jets gang. The hero, Tony, a former member of the Jets falls in love with Maria, the sister of the leader of the Sharks. The sophisticated music and the extended dance scenes, focussing on the social problems marked a turning point in musical theatre. The film starred Natalie Wood and Richard Beymer.

FASHION

CHANGING FASHION

It was a decade of three parts for fashion. The first years were reminiscent of the fifties, conservative and restrained, classic in style and design. Jackie Kennedy, the President's glamorous wife, was very influential with her tailored suit dresses and pill box hats, white pearls and kitten heels.

The hairdresser was of extreme importance. Beehive coiffures worn by the likes of Dusty Springfield and Brigitte Bardot were imitated by women of all ages and Audrey Hepburn popularised the high bosom, sleeveless dress. Whilst low, square toed shoes were high fashion, 'on the street', stilettos rivalled them.

THE MODS

In the mid-60s, the look had become sleeker and more modern. The lines were form-fitting but didn't try to accentuate curves. There were brighter colours and for the young, the Mod style.

Male mods took on a smooth, sophisticated look that included tailor-made suits with narrow lapels, thin ties, button-down collar shirts and wool jumpers.

The pea coat and Chelsea boots looked very 'London'. The Beatles were leading the way, hair started to grow longer, and trousers lost the baggy, comfortable fit of the 1950's.

For girls, shift dresses and mini skirts became shorter and shorter, worn with flat shoes or 'go go boots', short hair with eyebrow brushing fringes, and little makeup, just a pale lipstick and false eyelashes.

Slender models like Jean Shrimpton and Twiggy exemplified the look and new, exciting designers emerged such as Mary Quant. Television shows like 'Ready Steady Go!' showed their audiences at home, what they should be wearing.

IN THE 1960s

THE HIPPIES

For the young, jeans were becoming ubiquitous both for men and women, skin-tight drainpipes through to the flared bottoms of the late years. London had taken over from Paris to become the fashion centre of the world and in contrast to the beginning of the decade, the end was the exact opposite.

Bright, swirling colours. Psychedelic, tie-dye shirts, long hair and beards were commonplace. Individualism was the word and mini skirts were worn alongside brightly coloured and patterned tunics with flowing long skirts.

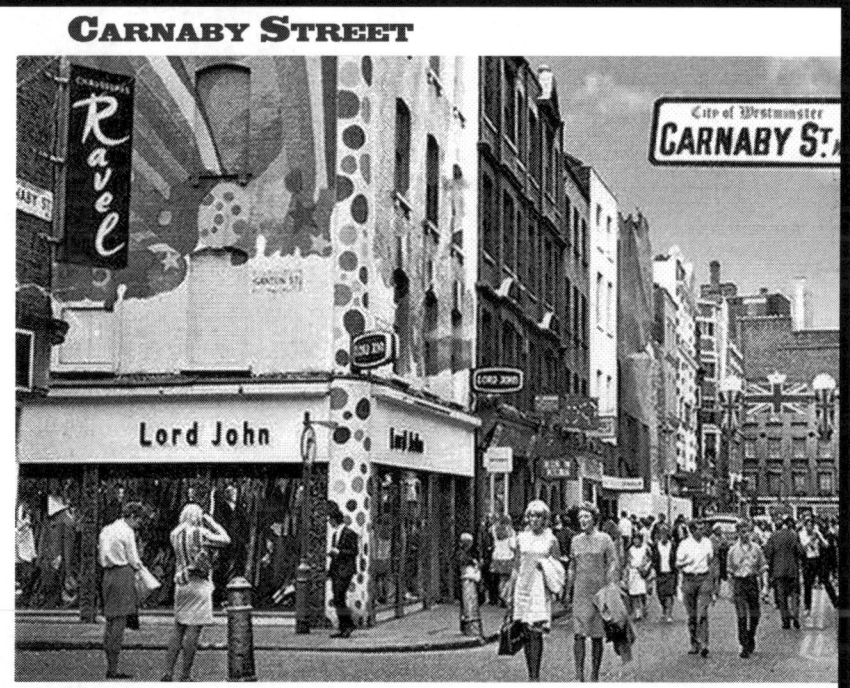

CARNABY STREET

By 1967, Carnaby Street was popular with followers of the mod and hippie styles. Many fashion designers, such as Mary Quant, Lord John and Irvine Sellars, had premises there, and underground music bars, such as the Roaring Twenties, opened in the surrounding streets.

Bands such as the Small Faces, The Who and The Rolling Stones appeared in the area, to work at the legendary Marquee Club round the corner in Wardour Street, to shop, and to socialise. The Street became one of the coolest destinations associated with 1960s Swinging London.

LEISURE

THE PACKAGE HOLIDAY

By the mid-sixties, the traditional British seaside holiday, sandcastles, donkey rides, sticks of rock and fish and chips on the beach was gradually giving way to the new and exciting Package Holiday in the sun.

Tour operators began taking plane loads of holidaymakers abroad, almost exclusively to Europe and to Spain in particular. Hotels were springing up everywhere, often obscuring the 'exotic views' that the tourists were promised and were basic with rather simple local fare, which even then was not to the taste of a large majority. Restaurants flourished with 'Full English Breakfast' posters displayed all over the windows, tea and beer were in demand.

By the end of the decade, Luton Airport, a favourite with the tour firms, had flights arriving back every hour full of sunburnt Brits wearing sombreros and clutching Spanish donkeys and maracas.

A cold British beach holiday was replaced for many by cheap package holidays to sunny Spain.

"LET'S GO FOR A CHINESE"

A 'Greasy Spoon'
A cheese-pineapple hedgehog

In the early 1960s, eating out was expensive and apart from 'greasy spoon' cafes, or a packet of salted crisps at a pub, dining out was limited to formal restaurants. However, with a rise in immigrants from Asia, Chinese and Indian restaurants were springing up and their relatively affordable and tasty food became so popular that Vesta brought out their first 'foreign convenience' foods, the Vesta Curries and Vesta Chow Mein.

A cheaper alternative was inviting friends to eat at home, and the dinner party boomed from the end of the decade. Pre-dinner drinks were often served with cubes of tinned pineapple and cheddar cheese on sticks, stuck into half a tinfoil covered grapefruit to look like a hedgehog – the height of 60s sophistication! The main course might feature the fashionable 'spaghetti bolognese', and 'Blue Nun', Mateus Rosé or Chianti wine, adding a hint of sophistication to the new 'smart' set's evening.

In The 1960s

Teenage Leisure

The 60's became the era for the teenager, but it started off with the same disciplines as the fifties. At school the teachers commanded respect and gave out punishment when it was not given. Parents could determine when and where their children could be out of house, gave sons and daughters chores to do and families ate together and watched television together.

Scouts and Guides were still very popular and a natural progression from the years as Cubs and Brownies and Outward Bounding or working for the Duke of Edinburgh Awards remained popular for many, but as the decade wore on, the lure of the new found freedom for the young was hard for many to overcome. Coffee bars became the place to meet, drink coffee or chocolate, listen to the latest hits on the juke box and talk with friends. The political climate influenced them, they demonstrated in the streets against the Vietnam War, for civil rights and to 'Ban the Bomb'. They developed the 'hippie' point of view, advocating non-violence and love, and by the end of the decade, "Make Love not War" was the 'flower children's' mantra.

Outdoor music festivals sprang up all over the country and thousands of, usually mud-caked, teenagers gathered to listen to their favourite artists, rock concerts played to packed houses and the young experimented with marijuana and LSD. Psychedelic art was incorporated into films, epitomised by the Beatles' 'Yellow Submarine'.

Music

1960 **Poor Me by Adam Faith**, a teen idol, reached number 1 and stayed there for two weeks whilst his previous number 1 hit, **What Do You Want** was still in the top ten. The Everly Brothers, the American rock duo, had their fifth number 1 with **Cathy's Clown**. Their first was Bye Bye Love in 1957. A surprise number 1 for four weeks was by Lonnie Donnegan, the skiffle singer, with **My Old Man's a Dustman.**

1961 **Wooden Heart** sung by Elvis Presley stayed at number 1 for six weeks and became the best-selling UK single of the year. Johnny Leyton had a three-week number 1 with **Johnny Remember Me** in August and it returned to the number 1 spot again at the end of September. Teenage singer and actress Helen Shapiro, had her second number one, **Walkin' Back to Happiness**, whilst still only fifteen.

1962 The top selling single of the year was by the Australian singer, Frank Ifield. **I Remember You** was sung in a yodelling, country-music style.
Acker Bilk's **Stranger on the Shore** becomes the first British recording to reach the number 1 spot on the US Billboard Hot 100.
The Rolling Stones make their debut at London's Marquee Club, opening for Long John Baldry.

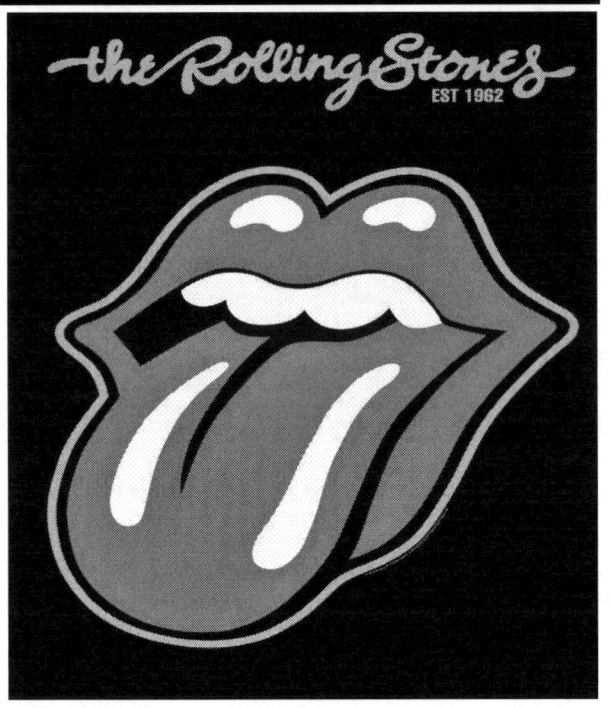

1962: The Rolling Stones make their debut at London's Marquee Club playing the rock n' roll of Chuck Berry and Bo Diddley.

1963 The Beatles have three number 1's in the UK charts in their first year. **From Me to You**, **She Loves You** and **I Want to Hold Your Hand.** Their debut album, **Please Please Me**, reaches the top of the album charts.
Produced by Phil Spector, The Crystals have a hit with **And Then He Kissed Me**
How Do You Do What You Do to Me, the debut single by Liverpudlian band Gerry and the Pacemakers, stays at number 1 for three weeks in April.

1964 The Hollies, the Merseybeat group founded by school friends Allan Clarke and Graham Nash, reach number 2 in the UK charts with **Just One Look**, a cover of the song by Doris Troy in the US.
Originally written by Burt Bacharach for Dionne Warwick, **Anyone Who Had a** Heart, sung by Cilla Black, became a UK number 1 for three weeks and was also the fourth best-selling single of 1964 in the UK, with sales of around 950,000 copies.

"The Fab Four", John Lennon, Paul McCartney, George Harrison and Ringo Star were the ultimate pop phenomenon of the '60s.

IN THE 1960s

1965 Unchained Melody by The Righteous Brothers, with a solo by Bobby Hatfield becomes a jukebox standard. **Its Not Unusual** sung by Tom Jones becomes an international hit after being promoted by the offshore, pirate radio station, Radio Caroline. **Get Off of My Cloud** by The Rolling Stones was written by Mick Jagger and Keith Richards as a single to follow their previous hit of the year, **(I Can't Get No) Satisfaction**.

1966 Nancy Sinatra with **These Boots Are Made for Walkin'** reaches number 1.
Good Vibrations sung by The Beach Boys, becomes an immediate hit both sides of the Atlantic.
Ike and Tina Turner released **River Deep, Mountain High** and their popularity soars in the UK after a tour with The Rolling Stones.

1967 Waterloo Sunset by The Kinks, written by Ray Davies, reached number 2 in the British charts and was a top 10 hit in Australia, New Zealand and most of Europe. In North America, it failed to chart.
A Whiter Shade of Pale the debut single by Procul Harem stays at number 1 for eight weeks.
Sandie Shaw wins the Eurovision Song Contest with **Puppet on a String**.

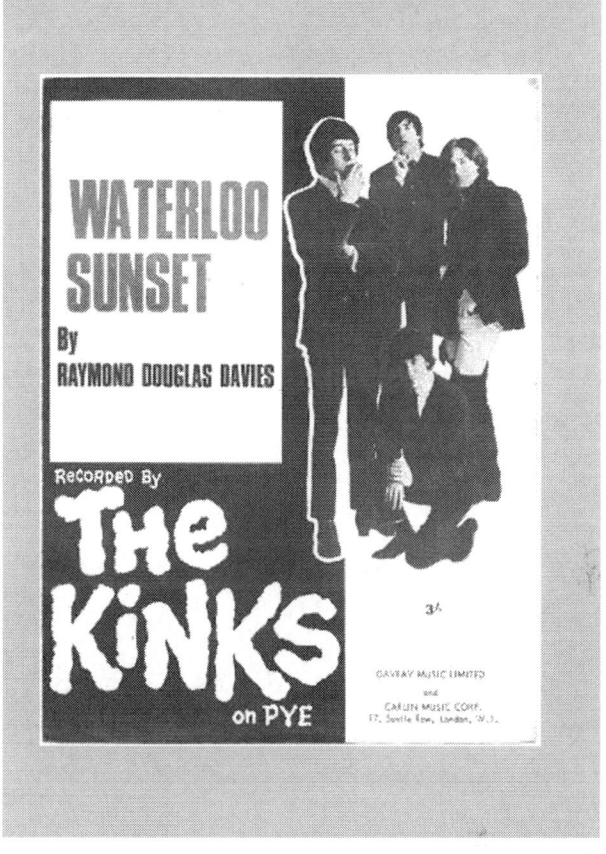

1968 Dusty Springfield's **Son of a Preacher Man** was her last top thirty hit until her collaboration with The Pet Shop Boys in 1987. In 1994, **Preacher Man** was included in Tarantino's film 'Pulp Fiction'.
Manfred Mann has a resounding success with **Mighty Quinn**, their third UK number 1 and third hit singing a song written by Bob Dylan.
The comedy group The Scaffold's record, **Lily the Pink** released in November became number 1 for the four weeks over the Christmas holidays.

1969 Where Do You Go To (My Lovely)? by the British singer-songwriter Peter Sarstedt stayed at number 1 for four weeks.
I Heard It Through the Grapevine was written in 1966 and recorded by Gladys Knight and the Pips. However, it was the version by Marvin Gaye that took the number 1 spot in the UK for three weeks and became the biggest hit single on the Motown label.
Je t'aime... moi non plus was written in 1967 for Brigitte Bardot but Serge Gainsbourg and Jane Birkin recorded the best known version and the duet reached number 1 in the UK. It was banned in several countries due to its overtly sexual content.

43

SCIENCE AND NATURE

THE LONDON SMOG

Britain still experienced "pea-soupers" in the 60's and in December 1962, London suffered under a choking blanket of smog. After three days, the noxious layer spread all over the country.

Smog is a concentration of smoke particles and other substances such as sulphur dioxide, combined with fog in conditions of low temperature, high pressure and lack of wind. Visibility was reduced such that a light could only be seen at 50ft and in spite of people covering their faces with scarves, surgical masks or handkerchiefs, the overwhelming smell of sulphur and coal smoke left an unpleasant metallic taste in the mouth and irritated eyes and noses. Bronchitis increased significantly and it is estimated that, in Greater London alone, there were 700 deaths in total.

In 1962, the Duke of Edinburgh was in New York for the inaugural dinner of the US branch of the World Wildlife Fund, first set up in Zurich in 1961, and warned his audience that our descendants could be forced to live in a world where the only living creature would be man himself -*"always assuming,"* he said, *"that we don't destroy ourselves as well in the meantime."*

In his speech, the Duke described poachers who were threatening extermination of many big game animals in Africa as "killers for profit … the get-rich-at-any-price mob." African poachers, he said, were killing off the rhinoceros to get its horn for export to China, *"where, for some incomprehensible reason, they seem to think it acts as an aphrodisiac."* The Duke also criticised the status seekers – people "like the eagle chasers". The bald eagle in North America was being chased and killed by people in light aeroplanes who seem to think it smart to own its feathers and claws.

"What is needed, above all now," he said, *"are people all over the world who understand the problem and really care about it. People who have the courage to see that the conservation laws are obeyed."*

DUKE OF EDINBURGH LAUNCHES WORLD WILDLIFE FUND

IN THE 1960s

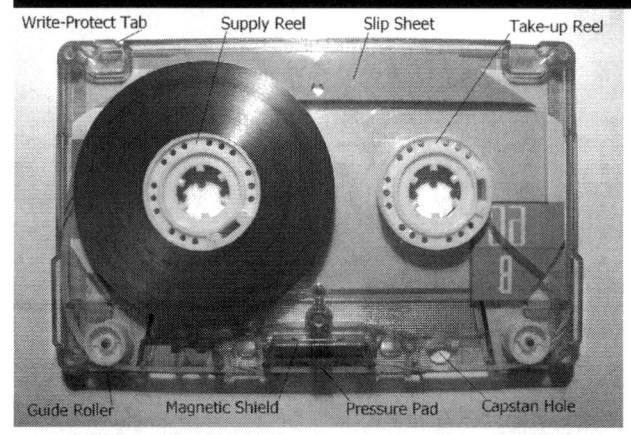

THE CASSETTE TAPE

The cassette tape was first developed by Philips in Belgium in 1962. These two small spools inside its plastic case, which wind magnetic-coated film on which the audio content is stored and pass it from one side to the other, meant music could now be recorded and shared by everyone.

Up until now, music was typically recorded on vinyl which needed a record player, or on reel-to-reel recorders which were comparatively expensive and difficult to use and neither of which were portable. The cassette player allowed individuals to record their favourite songs easily and also take their music with them "on-the-go". Music lovers soon learned how to create their own mixed tapes, for themselves or to share with friends.

More than 3 billion tapes were sold between 1962 and 1988.

THE ABERFAN DISASTER

On 21 October 1966, the worst mining-related disaster in British history took place in Aberfan, in South Wales. Coal was mined there for domestic heating and the waste was dumped at the top of the valley on land of no economic value. But crucially, it was tipped on highly porous sandstone which overlaid at least one natural spring.

During October 1966 heavy rainfall led to a build-up of water within this tip and caused it to collapse. With a deafening roar, 107 cu m of black slurry turned into an avalanche. The deluge leapt over the old railway embankment into the village where destroyed 18 houses and Pant Glas Junior School together with part of the neighbouring County Secondary School.

In total, 144 lives were lost, 116 of them children, 109 of these were aged between seven and ten and died in their classrooms on the last day before half term. Of the 28 adults who died, five were primary school teachers.

The official inquiry placed the blame entirely on the National Coal Board.

Sport

1960 - 1969

1960 In tennis, Rod Laver wins his first grand slam title as a 21-year-old taking the **Australian Open**.
Jack Brabham wins the **F1 driver's championship** for the second straight time.

1961 **Five Nations Championship** (now 6 Nations) rugby series is won by France.
Tottenham Hotspur beat Leicester City 2-0 in the **FA Cup Final**.

1962 Sonny Liston knocks out Floyd Pattison after two minutes into the first round of the "Boxing World Title" fight in Chicago.

1963 Mill House, at 18 hands, known as 'The Big Horse', wins the **Cheltenham Gold Cup**.

1964 The **Tour de France** is won by Jacques Anquetil of France, the first cyclist to win the Tour five times. 1957 and 1961-64.

1965 At the **Masters** in Atlanta, Jack Nicklaus shoots a record 17 under par to win the tournament.
In the **FA Cup Final** at Wembley, Liverpool beats Leeds United 2-1.

1966 England defeat Germany to win the **FIFA World Cup**

1967 Defending champion Billie Jean King defeats Ann Haydon-Jones in the **Wimbledon Women's Singles Championship**.
The New York Yacht Club retains the **America's Cup** when 'Intrepid' beat the Australian challenger 'Dame Pattie', 4 races to 1.

1968 English International cricketer Basil D'Oliveira, of 'Cape Coloured' background, is excluded from the **MCC South African tour** side, leading to turmoil in the world of cricket.

1969 **The Grand National** is won by 12-year-old Highland Wedding by 12 lengths.

1966 FIFA World Cup

On July 30th, England and West Germany lined up at Wembley to determine the winner of the 'Jules Rimet Trophy', the prize for winning the World Cup. England won 4-2 after extra time and the match is remembered for Geoff Hurst's hat-trick and the controversial third goal awarded to England by the referee and linesman.

In addition to an attendance of 96,924 at the stadium, the British television audience peaked at 32.3 million viewers, making it the UK's most-watched television event ever.

It was the first occasion that England had hosted, or won, the World Cup and was to remain their only major tournament win. It was also the nation's last final at a major international football tournament for 55 years, until 2021 when England reached the Euro Final but lost to Italy after a penalty shootout.

IN THE 1960s

1964 OLYMPIC GAMES

In 1964, the first Olympic Games to be held in Asia, took place in Japan during October to avoid the city's midsummer heat and humidity and the September typhoon season. It marked many milestones in the history of the modern Games; a cinder running track was used for the last time in the athletics events, whilst a fibreglass pole was used for the first time in the pole-vaulting competition. These Games were also the last occasion that hand timing by stopwatch was used for official timing.

25 world records were broken and 52 of a possible 61 Olympic records were also broken. Ethiopian runner Abebe Bikila won his second consecutive Olympic marathon. Bob Hayes won the men's 100 metres and then anchored the US 400 metre relay team to a world record victory. Peter Snell, the New Zealand middle-distance runner, won both the 800 and 1500 metres, the only man to have done so in the same Olympics since 1920. Ann Packer of Britain made a record-breaking debut winning gold in the 800 metres and silver in the 400 metres.

Peter Snell, winning the 1500 metres.

CASSIUS CLAY HEAVYWEIGHT CHAMPION OF THE WORLD

In 1964, Cassius Clay, later this year to be known as Muhammad Ali, fought and gained Sonny Liston's title of Heavyweight Champion of the World. The big fight took place in Miami Beach in February.

Liston was an intimidating fighter and Clay was the 7-1 under-dog, but still he engaged in taunting his opponent during the build-up to the fight, dubbing him *"the big ugly bear"*, stating *"Liston even smells like a bear"* and claiming, *"After I beat him, I'm going to donate him to the zoo!"*

The result of the fight was a major upset as Clay's speed and mobility kept him out of trouble and in the third round hit Liston with a combination that opened a cut under his left eye and eventually, Liston could not come out for the seventh round.

A triumphant Clay rushed to the edge of the ring and, pointing to the ringside press, shouted: *"Eat your words!"* adding the words he was to live up to for the rest of his life, *"I am the greatest!"*

Transport

Trolleybuses were taken out of service in London in May having served since 1931.

How luxurious can an Austin Seven get?

The revolutionary Mini was the fastest selling small car in Britain in the 60s. Despite the promise of the adverts early models were slow and unreliable and although promoted as a luxury family car, it was uncomfortable and cramped.

The Vickers VC10

The 60's produced Britain's biggest airliner to date, the four jet Vickers VC10. With a towering tailplane, high as a four-storey house, the airliner weighed 150 tons fully loaded and was 158ft long. In service with BOAC and other airlines from the end of 1963 until 1981, the plane could carry 150 passengers at flew at 600mph over distances exceeding 4,000 miles. From 1965 they were also used as strategic air transports for the RAF.

Cars Of The Decade

The importance of personal transport increased dramatically during the Sixties and three of the images inextricably linked with the decade are the three-wheeler 'bubble car', the sleek, sexy, elongated E-type Jaguar and VW Camper Van.

IN THE 1960s

MODS AND ROCKERS
SCOOTERS v MOTOR BIKES

Mods and Rockers were two rival British youth sub-cultures of the 1960's with a tendency to riot on Brighton beach.

They had very different outlooks: The Mods thought of themselves as sophisticated, stylish and in touch with the times. The motor cycling centred Rockers thought the Mods effeminate snobs!

They had very different appearances: Mods centred on fashion and wore suits or other clean-cut outfits. The Rockers wore black leather jackets and motorcycle boots or sometimes, 'brothel creeper' shoes.

They had very different tastes in music. The Mods favoured Soul and African American R&B. The Rockers went for Rock 'n Roll.

So not surprisingly, they had very different tastes in transport.

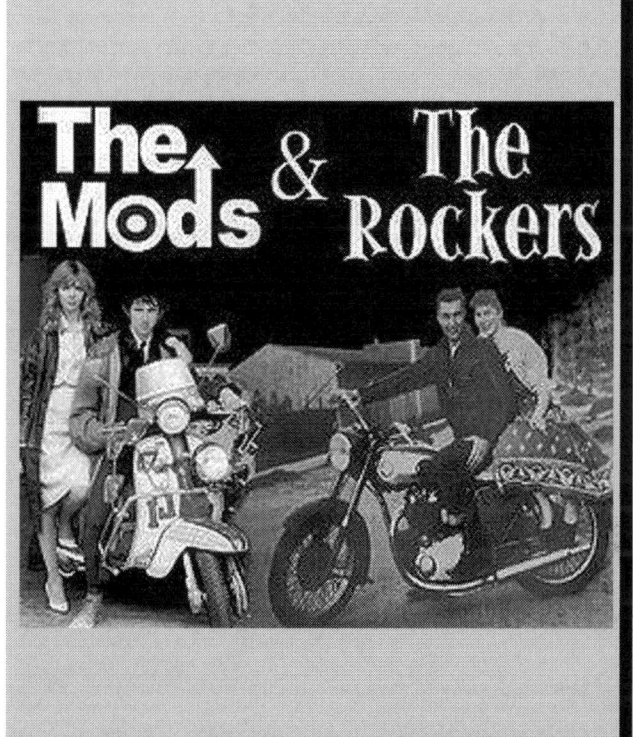

THE HOVERCRAFT

The great British invention of the decade was the Hovercraft. It was developed by Briton, Sir Christopher Cockerell. Saunders Roe, the flying boat firm at Cowes on the Isle of Wight built the prototype SR.N1, 20ft craft which first took to the seas in July 1959, crossing the English Channel from Calais to Dover in two hours with the inventor onboard. In 1961 hovercraft skirts were introduced to the design which provided far greater performance abilities and sea keeping.

The Hovercraft was a revolution in sea travel and the 1960's saw a fleet of craft crossing from the south coast to the Isle of Wight. They are now used throughout the world as specialised transports in disaster relief, coastguard, military and survey applications, as well as for sport or passenger service.

THE MAJOR NEWS STORIES

1970 - 1974

1970:
Jan: The age of majority for most legal purposes was reduced from 21 to 18 under terms of the Family Law Reform Act 1969.

Mar: Ian Smith declares Rhodesia a Republic and the British government refuses to recognise the new state.

1971:
Feb: Decimal Day. The UK and the Republic of Ireland both change to decimal currency.

Mar: The 'Daily Sketch', Britain's oldest tabloid newspaper is absorbed by the 'Daily Mail' after 62 years.

1972:
June: The 'Watergate' scandal begins in Richard Nixon's administration in the US.

Sep: The school leaving age in the UK was raised from 15 to 16 for pupils leaving at the end of the academic year.

1973:
Jan: The United Kingdom joins the European Economic Community, later to become the EU.

Sep: The IRA detonate bombs in Manchester and Victoria Station London and two days later, Oxford St. and Sloane Square.

1974:
Jan: Until March, the 3-day week is introduced by the Conservative Government to conserve electricity during the miners' strike.

Nov: 21 people are killed and 182 injured when the IRA set bombs in two Birmingham pubs.

1974: McDonald's open their first UK restaurant in South London. The traditional café was losing out, slow ordering and service with food served at tables was not as appealing as the clean, fast service and lower prices of this new fast food.

1974: In February, Harold Wilson becomes Prime Minister for the second time (first 1964-70) with a minority Government after Edward Heath resigns having failed to clinch a coalition with the Liberals. In the second general election of the year in October, Labour win with a majority of only 3 seats.

OF THE 1970s

1975 - 1979

In June and July 1976, the UK experienced a heat wave. Temperatures peak at 35.9° and the whole country suffers a severe drought. Forest fires broke out, crops failed, and reservoirs dried up causing serious water shortages. The heatwave also produced swarms of ladybirds across the south and east.

On the 7th June, 1977, more than one million people lined the streets of London to watch the Queen and Prince Phillip lead a procession in the golden state coach, to St Paul's at the start of a week of the Queen's Silver Jubilee celebrations – 25 years on the throne. People all over the country held street or village parties to celebrate, more than 100,000 cards were received by the Queen and 30,000 Jubilee medals were given out.

1975:
Feb: Margaret Thatcher defeats Edward Heath to become the first female leader of the Conservative Party.

Apr: The Vietnam War ends with the Fall of Saigon to the Communists. South Vietnam surrenders unconditionally.

1976:
Mar: Harold Wilson announces his resignation as Prime Minister and James Callaghan is elected to the position in April.

Oct: The Intercity 125 high speed passenger train is introduced. Initially Paddington to Bristol and south Wales.

1977:
Jan: Jimmy Carter is sworn in as the 39th President of the United States, succeeding Gerald Ford.

Sep: Freddie Laker launches his 'Skytrain' with a single fare, Gatwick to New York, at £59 compared to £189.

1978:
Aug: Louise Brown becomes the world's first human born 'in vitro fertilisation' – test tube baby.

Nov: An industrial dispute shuts down The Times newspaper – until November 1979.

1979:
Mar: Airey Neave, politician and WW2 veteran, is blown up in the House of Commons carpark by the Irish National Liberation Army.

May: Margaret Thatcher becomes the first female Prime Minister of the United Kingdom. The Conservatives win a 43 seat majority.

THE HOME

Increasing Comfort and Prosperity

Homes became brighter and more comfortable in the 1970's. Teenagers could lie on the 'impossible to clean', loopy shag pile carpet watching films on VHS video cassettes or watch live programmes on the family's colour television set.

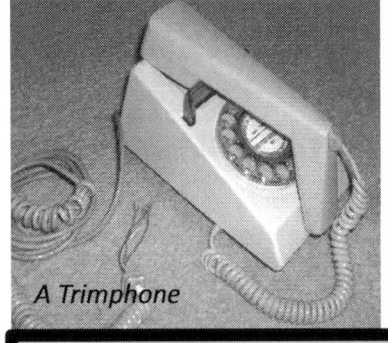

A Trimphone

The ubiquitous macramé owl, or plant holder complete with trailing spider plant, might dangle in the corner adjacent to the bulky, stone faced, rustic fireplace. Bathroom suites were often Avocado green and 'downstairs loos' were a statement of the houseowners ideals! If you were one of the 35% of households in Britain to own a telephone, you could catch up with friends and family on the new 'warbling' Trimphone, maybe sitting on your bright, floral covered couch.

Labour Saving Devices

The previous decade had been prosperous and the advances in technology continued such that by the 1970s, most households had many labour-saving devices. Sales of freezers rose rapidly in the 70s and by 1974, one in ten households had a freezer - mainly full of peas, chips and fish fingers but also ice cream, previously a rare treat, and in large quantities. Bulk buying food meant less time shopping and the Magimix food processor which added a choice of blades and attachments to a standard liquidiser, made home cooking more adventurous.

IN THE 1970s

Teenage Home Entertainment

Teenagers covered their bedroom walls with posters of their favourite bands and actors, ranging from Rod Stewart and the Boomtown Rats to Olivia Newton-John and Robert Redford. The lucky ones listening to top ten singles on their own stereo record deck which had replaced the old Dansette player.

If they wanted to play the new video games, they typically went to an arcade, but in 1975, Atari PONG was released, the first commercially successful video game you could play at home on your television. Based on a simple two-dimensional graphical representation of a tennis-like game, two players used paddles to hit a ball back and forth on a black and white screen. It captivated audiences and its success influenced developers to invent more and increasingly sophisticated games for the home market.

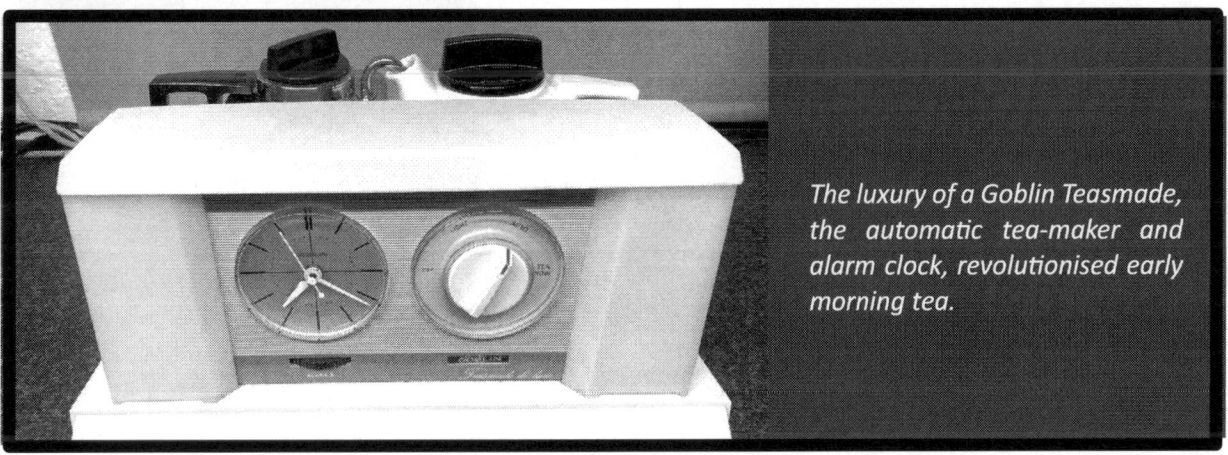

The luxury of a Goblin Teasmade, the automatic tea-maker and alarm clock, revolutionised early morning tea.

Art and Culture

1970 - 1974

1970 Laurence Olivier becomes the first actor to be made a Lord. He is given a life peerage in the Queen's Birthday Honours list.
The first Glastonbury Festival was held, called the Worthy Farm Pop Festival. About 1500 attended.

1971 Coco Chanel, the French fashion designer died. (Born 1883)
The 'Blue Peter' presenters buried a time capsule in the grounds of BBC Television Centre, due to be opened on the first episode in 2000.
Mr Tickle, the first of the Mr Men books is published.

1972 'Jesus Christ Superstar', the Tim Rice & Andrew Lloyd Webber musical opens in the West End.
John Betjeman is appointed Poet Laureate.

1973 The British Library is established by merger of the British Museum Library & the National Lending Library for Science & Technology.
Series 1 of the BBC sitcom, 'Last of the Summer Wine' begins. There are eventually, 31 series.

1974 'Tinker, Tailor, Soldier, Spy' the first of John Le Carré's novel featuring the ageing spymaster, George Smiley, is published.
The Terracotta Army of Qin Shi Huang, thousands of life-size clay models of soldiers, horses and chariots, is discovered at Xi'an in China.

Milton Keynes Shopping Centre

1975 - 1979

1975 Donald Coggan is enthroned as the Archbishop of Canterbury.
Bill Gates and Paul Allen found Microsoft in Albuquerque, New Mexico.

1976 Trevor Nunn's memorable production of 'Macbeth' opens at Stratford-upon-Avon, with Ian McKellan and Judi Dench in the lead roles.
The Royal National Theatre on the South Bank opens.
Agatha Christie's last novel, Sleeping Murder, a Miss Marple story is published posthumously.

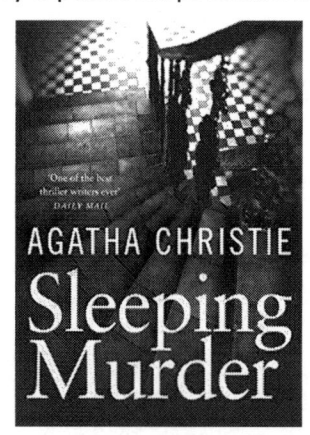

1977 Luciano Pavarotti makes his television debut singing in Puccini's La Boheme in the television debut of 'Live from the Met'.
Mike Leigh's satire on the aspirations and tastes of the new middle class emerging in the 70's, 'Abigail's Party', opened at the Hampstead Theatre starring Alison Steadman.

1978 The Andrew Lloyd Webber musical 'Evita' opens in London.
The arcade video game, 'Space Invaders' is released.

1979 Margaret Thatcher opens the new Central Milton Keynes Shopping Centre, the largest indoor shopping centre in Britain.
Anthony Blunt, British art historian and former Surveyor of the Queen's Pictures, in exposed as a double agent for the Soviets during WW2.
The Sony Walkman, portable cassette player is released.

IN THE 1970s

Pavarotti at the Met.

It was in his third season at the Metropolitan Opera House in New York that Luciano Pavarotti, the operatic tenor, would skyrocket to stardom. The company imported Covent Garden's production of Donizetti's *La Fille du Régiment* in 1972 as a vehicle for Joan Sutherland. The great Australian diva enjoyed a huge triumph, but the surprise for the audience was the young Italian tenor by her side who shared an equal part in the phenomenal success. This was the historic first Met performance telecast live on PBS as part of the long-running series that continues to the present day.

The Terracotta Army

'The Qin Tomb Terracotta Warriors and Horses' was constructed between 246-206BC as an afterlife guard for China's First Emperor, Qin Shihuang, from whom, China gets its name. He ordered it built to remember the army he led to triumph over other warring states, and to unite China.

The tomb and the army were all made by hand by some 700,000 artisans and labourers, and comprises thousands of life-size soldiers, each with different facial features and expressions, clothing, hairstyles and gestures, arranged in battle array.

All figures face east, towards the ancient enemies of Qin State, in rectangular formations and three separate vaults include rows of kneeling and standing archers, chariot war configurations and mixed forces of infantry, horse drawn chariots plus numerous soldiers armed with long spears, daggers and halberds.

Films

1970 - 1974

1970 Love Story, was the biggest grossing film a sentimental, tearjerker with the oft-quoted tagline, "Love means never having to say you're sorry." Nominated for the Academy Awards Best Picture, it was beaten by **Patton** which won 7 major titles that year.

1971 The Oscar winner was **The French Connection** with Gene Hackman as a New York police detective, Jimmy 'Popeye' Doyle, chasing down drug smugglers. Hackman was at the peak of his career in the 70's.

1972 Francis Ford Coppola's gangster saga, **The Godfather** became the highest grossing film of its time and helped drive a resurgence in the American film industry.

1973 Glenda Jackson won Best Actress for her role in **A Touch of Class.** She revealed that she was approached for the part by the director after appearing in the 1971 'Antony & Cleopatra' sketch on the Morecambe & Wise show. After she won, Eric Morecambe sent her a telegram saying, "Stick with us and we will get you another one".

1974 New films this year included **The Godfather Part II,** which won the Oscar, **Blazing Saddles** the comedy western and the disaster film, **The Towering Inferno** starring Paul Newman and Steve McQueen.

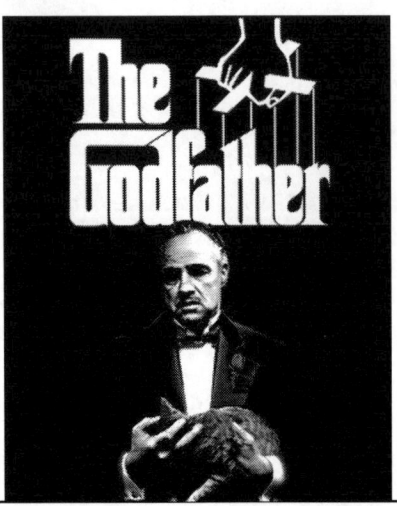

1975 - 1979

1975 One Flew Over the Cuckoo's Nest, an allegorical film set in a mental hospital, starring Jack Nicholson, beat tough competition for Best Picture from Spielberg's **Jaws** and Altman's **Nashville.**

1976 Jodi Foster won an Oscar in Martin Scorsese's gritty film **Taxi Driver** which examines alienation in urban society but it was Sylvester Stallone's **Rocky** that carried off the Best Picture award.

1977 Annie Hall from Woody Allen, the winner of Best Picture is a masterpiece of witty and quotable one-liners.

1978 The Vietnam War is examined through the lives of three friends from a small steel-mill town before, during and after their service in **The Deer Hunter**. A powerful and disturbing film.

1979 In this year's Best Picture, **Kramer v Kramer** there is a restaurant scene where Dustin Hoffman throws his wine glass at the wall. Only the cameraman was forewarned, Meryl Streep's shocked reaction was genuine!

IN THE 1970s

Star Wars

Star Wars all began with George Lucas's eponymous film in 1977. The epic space fantasy, telling the adventures of characters "A long time ago in a galaxy far, far away", and this first film was a world beater in special effects technology using new computerised and digital effects. It rapidly became a phenomenon, Luke Skywalker, Jedi Knights, Princess Leia and Darth Vader becoming household names. An immensely valuable franchise grew up to include the films, television series, video games, books, comics and theme parks which now amounts to billions of dollars and the film introduced the phrase "May the Force be with you" into common usage.

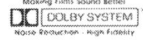

Apocalypse Now

Joseph Conrad's book 'Heart of Darkness' was the inspiration for producer and director Francis Ford Coppola's psychological film, a metaphor for the madness and folly of war itself for a generation of young American men. Beautiful, with symbolic shots showing the confusion, violence and fear of the nightmare of the Vietnam War, much of it was filmed on location in the Philippines where expensive sets were destroyed by severe weather, a typhoon called 'Olga', Marlon Brando showed up on set overweight and completely unprepared and Martin Sheen had a near-fatal heart attack.

This led to the film being two and a half times over budget and taking twice the number of scheduled weeks to shoot. When filming finally finished, the release was postponed several times as Coppola had six hours of film to edit. The helicopter attack scene with the 'Ride of the Valkyries' soundtrack is one of the most memorable film scenes ever.

Fashion

Women Wear the Trousers

It is often said that 1970s styles had no direction and were too prolific. French couture no longer handed down diktats of what we should be wearing, and the emerging street style was inventive, comfortable, practical for women or glamorous. It could be home-made, it was whatever you wanted it to be, and the big new trend was for gender neutral clothes, women wore trousers in every walk of life, trouser suits for the office, jeans at home and colourful, tight-fitting ones for in between. Trouser legs became wider and 'bell-bottoms', flared from the knee down, with bottom leg openings of up to twenty-six inches, made from denim, bright cotton and satin polyester, became mainstream. Increasingly 'low cut', they were teamed with platform soles or high cut boots until they could not flare anymore, and so, by the end of the decade they had gone, skin-tight trousers, in earth tones, greys, whites and blacks were much more in vogue.

And the Hot Pants

In the early 70s, women's styles were very flamboyant with extremely bright colours and, in the winter, long, flowing skirts and trousers *but* come the summer, come the Hot Pants. These extremely short shorts were made of luxury fabrics such as velvet and satin designed for fashionable wear, not the practical equivalents for sports or leisure, and they enjoyed great popularity until falling out of fashion in the middle of the decade. Teamed with skin-tight t-shirts, they were favourites for clubwear and principally worn by women, including Jacqueline Kennedy Onassis, Elizabeth Taylor and Jane Fonda, but they were also worn by some high-profile men, David Bowie, Sammy Davis Jnr and Liberace among them, although the shorts were slightly longer than the women's versions, but still shorter than usual. Chest hair, medallions, sideburns and strangely, tennis headbands, finished the look!

IN THE 1970s

These Boots Are Made For Walking

Boots were so popular in the early 1970s that even men were getting in on the action. It wasn't uncommon to see a man sporting 2" inch platform boots inspired by John Travolta in Saturday Night Fever. The trend was all about being sexy on the dance floor!

And Punk Was Not to Be Ignored

Emerging in the mid 70s in London as an anarchic and aggressive movement, a few hundred young people defined themselves as an anti-fashion urban youth street culture closely aligned to the music that became punk. They cut up old clothes from charity shops, destroyed the fabric and refashioned outfits in a manner intended to shock. Trousers were deliberately torn to reveal laddered tights and dirty legs and worn with heavy Doc Martens footwear, now seen on many young women too.

Safety pins and chains held bits of fabric together. Neck chains were made from padlocks and chain and even razor blades were used as pendants. Body piercings and studs, beginning with the three-stud earlobe, progressing to the ear outline embedded with ear studs, evolved to pins in eyebrows, cheeks, noses or lips and together with tattoos were the beginning of unisex fashion. All employed by male and female alike to offend. Vivienne Westwood and Malcolm McLaren quickened the style with her bondage shop "Sex", and his punk music group, the "Sex Pistols".

LEISURE

Saturday Morning TV

In the early 70s, Saturday mornings for many children still meant a trip to the cinema but with the advent of Saturday Morning Television, under instruction 'not to wake their parents', children could creep downstairs, switch on the box and stay entertained until lunchtime.

First, in 1974, came ITV's 'Tiswas', hosted by Chris Tarrant it was a chaotic blend of jokes, custard pies and buckets of water.

Then in 1976, the BBC introduced 'Swap Shop' with Noel Edmonds, Keith Chegwin and John Craven and a Saturday morning ritual was born. Nearly three hours of ground-breaking television using the 'phone-in' extensively for the first time on TV. The programme included music, competitions, cartoons and spontaneous nonsense from Edmonds. There was coverage of news and issues relevant to children, presented by 'Newsround's' John Craven but by far the most popular element of the show was the "Swaporama" open-air event, hosted by Chegwin. An outside broadcast unit would travel to different locations throughout the UK where sometimes as many as 2000 children would gather to swap their belongings with others.

Saturday Night Fever

Memories of Saturday night and Sunday morning in the discotheque. A mirror ball; strobe lights; 'four on the floor' rhythm; the throb of the bass drum; girls in Spandex tops with hot pants or vividly coloured, shiny, Lycra trousers with equally dazzling halter neck tops; boys in imitations of John Travolta's white suit from Saturday Night Fever risking life and limb on towering platform shoes.

These glamorous dancers, clad in glitter, metallic lame and sequins, gyrating as the music pounded out at the direction of the DJ, whirling energetically and glowing bright 'blue-white' under the ultra-violet lights as their owners 'strutted their stuff', perspiration running in rivulets down their backs.

The DJs, stars in their own right, mixed tracks by Donna Summer, the Bee Gees, Gloria Gaynor, Sister Sledge, Chic and Chaka Khan, as their sexy followers, fuelled by the night club culture of alcohol and drugs, changed from dancing the Hustle with their partners to the solo freestyle dancing of John Travolta.

IN THE 1970s

The Dangers of Leisure

In the 1970's the Government was intent on keeping us all – and particularly children – safe and continued producing the wartime Public Information Films, which were still scaring children witless!

1971: Children and Disused Fridges: Graphic warnings of children being suffocated in old fridges that, tempted by their playful imaginations, they want to climb into.

1973: Broken Glass: This film shows a boy running on the sand, ending abruptly before he steps on a broken glass bottle, the film urges people to use a bin or take their litter home with them.

1974: The Fatal Floor: This 30 second film had the message, "Polish a floor, put a rug on it, and you might as well set a man trap..."

1979: Play Safe – Frisbee: This film used chilling electronic music and frightening sound effects to highlight the potentially fatal combination of frisbees with electricity pylons and kites, fishing rods and radio-controlled planes.

1972: Teenagers – Learn to Swim:
A cartoon aimed at teenagers warns them to learn how to swim, or risk social embarrassment and failure to attract the opposite sex. The female character's illusion of her boyfriend 'Dave' being able 'to do anything' is shattered after she wishes they were at the seaside, where she discovers Dave can't swim. He in turn wishes he didn't 'keep losing me birds' after his girlfriend disappears with 'Mike' who 'swims like a fish'. Although the film is light-hearted in tone it was intended in part to help prevent accidents.

1975: Protect and Survive:
This was the title of a series of booklets and films made in the late 1970s and early 1980s, dealing with emergency planning for a nuclear war including the recognition of attack warning, fallout warning, and all-clear signals, the preparation of a home "fallout room" and the stockpiling of food, water, and other emergency supplies. In the opinion of some contemporary critics, the films *were deeply and surprisingly fatalistic in tone*!

Music

1970 - 1974

1970 Number 1 for 3 weeks, **Bridge Over Troubled Water** by Simon and Garfunkel became their 'signature song' selling over 6m copies worldwide. It also became one of the most performed songs of the 20th century, covered by over 50 artists.

1971 George Harrison's first release as a solo **My Sweet Lord** topped the charts for five weeks and became the best selling UK single of the year.
Rod Stewart had 7 No 1's this year including in October, the double sided hits, **Reason to Believe/Maggie May**

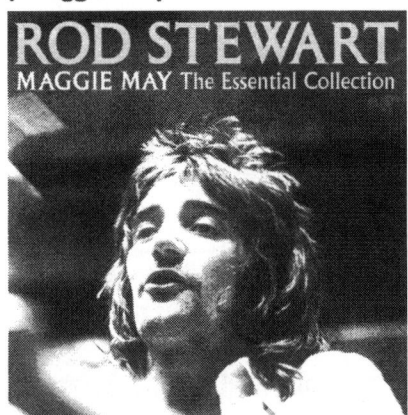

1972 A jingle, rewritten to become the hugely popular 'Buy the world a Coke' advert for the Coca Cola company, was re-recorded by The New Seekers as the full-length song, **I'd Like to Teach the World to Sing**, which stayed at No 1 for 4 weeks.

1973 Dawn featuring Tony Orlando had the bestselling single of 1973 with **"Tie a Yellow Ribbon Round the 'Ole Oak Tree"**, which spent four weeks at the top spot and lasted 11 weeks in the top ten.
Queen released their debut album, **"Queen"**. The Carpenters reached number 2 with **"Yesterday Once More"**.

1974 Waterloo, the winning song for Sweden in the Eurovision Song Contest began ABBA's journey to world-wide fame.
David Essex has his first No 1 with **Wanna Make You a Star** which spends 3 weeks at the top of the charts.

1975 - 1979

1975 Make Me Smile (Come Up and See Me) was a chart topper for Steve Harley & Cockney Rebel. **Bohemian Rhapsody** for Queen, stayed at the top for nine weeks.

1976 The Brotherhood of Man won the Eurovision Song Contest for Great Britain with **Save Your Kisses for Me**. It became the biggest-selling song of the year and remains one of the biggest-selling Eurovision winners ever.
Don't Go Breaking My Heart was the first No. 1 single in the UK for both Elton John and Kiki Dee.

1977 Actor David Soul, riding high on his success in Starsky & Hutch, had the No 1 spot for 4 weeks with **Don't Give Up on Us**.
Way Down was the last song to be recorded by Elvis Presley before his death and stayed at No 1 for 5 weeks.

1978 Kate Bush released her debut single, **Wuthering Heights,** which she had written aged 18 after watching Emily Brontë's Wuthering Heights on television and discovering she shared the author's birthday.
Spending five weeks at the top of the British charts, Boney M's **"Rivers of Babylon"** became the biggest selling single of the year, exceeding one million sales between May and June.

1979 Frequently recalled as a symbol of female empowerment, **I Will Surviv**e reached the top for Gloria Gaynor.
The Wall, Pink Floyd's rock opera was released, featuring all three parts of **Another Brick in the Wall. Part 2**, written as a protest against rigid schooling was No1 in Dec.

In The 1970s

The Decade in Numbers

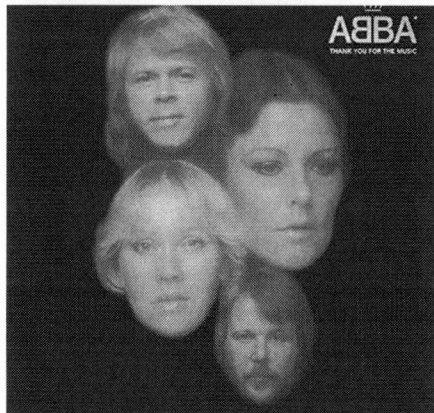

Most No1 Singles:
ABBA with seven.
Waterloo (1974);
Mamma Mia, Fernando and
Dancing Queen (all 1976);
Knowing Me Knowing You, The Name of the Game, (both 1977);
Take a Chance on Me (1978).

Most Weeks at No 1:
Bohemian Rhapsody by Queen; **Mull of Kintyre / Girl's School** by Wings; **You're the One That I Want** by John Travolta and Olivia Newton-John.

'Danny' and 'Sandy' Fever

Grease, the 1978 musical romantic comedy starring John Travolta (Danny) and Olivia Newton-John (Sandy) had phenomenal success. In June to August 1978, **You're the One That I Want** and in September to October, **Summer Nights**, locked up the number 1 position for a total of sixteen weeks.

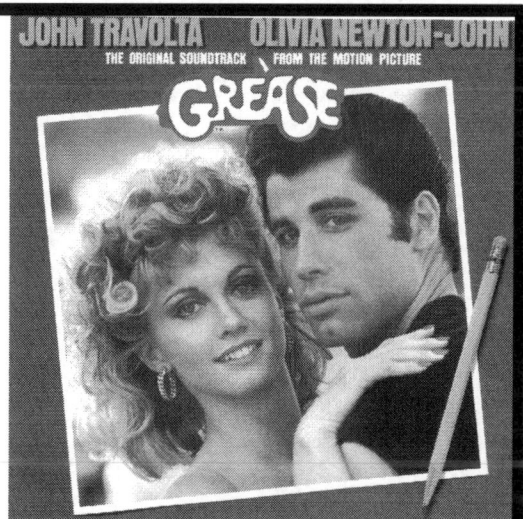

Hopelessly Devoted to You was nominated for an Oscar and John Travolta and Olivia Newton-John seemed to be constantly in the public conscience. Critically and commercially successful, the soundtrack album ended 1978 as the second best-selling album in the US, behind the soundtrack of the 1977 blockbuster **Saturday Night Fever,** which also starred John Travolta.

Science and Nature

Pocket Calculators

The first pocket calculators came onto the market towards the end of 1970. In the early 70s they were an expensive status symbol but by the middle of the decade, businessmen were quite used to working their sales figures out quickly whilst 'out of the office'.

Household accounts were made easy and children wished they could use them at school – not just to help with homework. Most early calculators performed only basic addition, subtraction, multiplication and division but the speed and accuracy, sometimes giving up to 12 digit answers, of the machine proved sensational.

In 1972, Hewlett Packard introduced the revolutionary HP-35 pocket calculator which, in addition to the basic operations, enabled advanced mathematical functions. It was the first scientific, hand-held calculator, able to perform a wide number of logarithmic and trigonometric functions, store intermediate solutions and utilise scientific notations.

With intense competition, prices of pocket calculators dropped rapidly, and the race was on to produce the smallest possible models. The target was to be no bigger than a credit card. Casio won the race.

The Miracle of IVF

In 1971, Patrick Steptoe, gynaecologist, Robert Edwards, biologist, and Jean Purdy, nurse and embryologist set up a small laboratory at the Kershaw's Hospice in Oldham which was to lead to the development of in vitro fertilisation and eventual birth of Louise Brown in 1978.

They developed a technique for retrieving eggs at the right time and fertilising them in the laboratory, believing that they could be implanted back in the uterus. It took more than 80 embryo transfers before the first successful pregnancy, and the birth of Louise, the first 'test-tube baby', heralded the potential happiness of infertile people and a bright future for British science and industry.

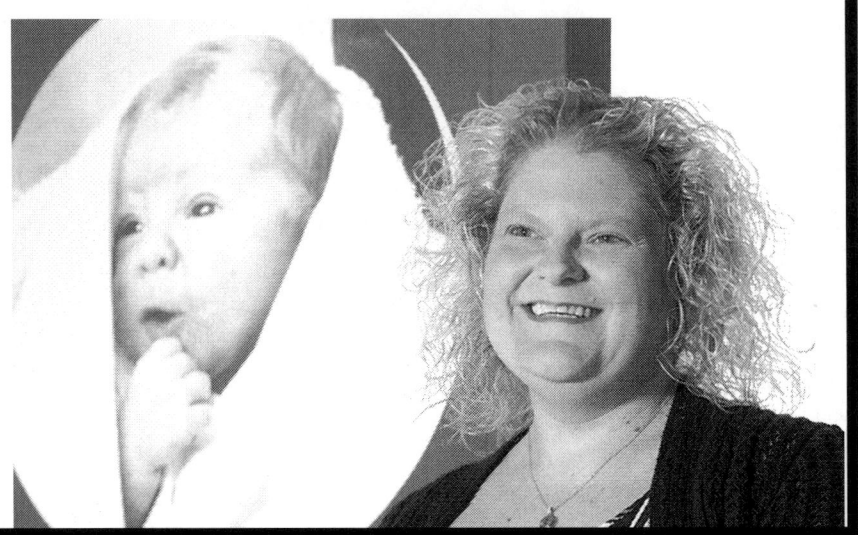

IN THE 1970s

"Houston We Have a Problem"

In April 1970, two days after the launch of Apollo 13, the seventh crewed mission in the Apollo space program and the third meant to land on the Moon, the NASA ground crew heard the now famous message, "Houston, we've had a problem." An oxygen tank had exploded, and the lunar landing was aborted leaving the astronauts in serious danger. The crew looped around the Moon and returned safely to Earth, their safe return being down to the ingenuity under pressure by the crew, commanded by Jim Lovell, together with the flight controllers and mission control. The crew experienced great hardship, caused by limited power, a chilly and wet cabin and a shortage of drinking water.

Even so, Apollo 13 set a spaceflight record for the furthest humans have travelled from Earth.

Tens of millions of viewers watched Apollo 13 splashdown in the South Pacific Ocean and the recovery by USS Iwo Jima.

The global campaigning network **Greenpeace** was founded in 1971 by Irving and Dorothy Stowe, environmental activists. The network now has 26 independent national or regional organisations in 55 countries worldwide.

Their stated goal is to ensure the ability of the earth to nurture life in all its diversity. To achieve this they "use non-violent, creative confrontation to expose global environmental problems, and develop solutions for a green and peaceful future". In detail to:

- Stop the planet from warming beyond 1.5° in order to prevent the most catastrophic impacts of the climate breakdown.
- Protect biodiversity in all its forms.
- Slow the volume of hyper-consumption and learn to live within our means.
- Promote renewable energy as a solution that can power the world.
- Nurture peace, global disarmament and non-violence.

Sport

1970 - 1974

1970 The thoroughbred 'Nijinsky', wins all three English Triple Crown Races: **The 2,000 Guineas** at Newmarket; **The Derby** at Epsom; the **St. Leger Stakes** at Doncaster and the Irish Derby. The first horse to do this in 35 years and not repeated as of 2021.

1971 Arsenal wins both the **First Division** title and the **FA Cup**, becoming the fourth team ever to win the double.
Jack Nicklaus wins his ninth major at the **PGA Championship**, the first golfer ever to win all four majors for the second time.

1972 At **Wimbledon**, Stan Smith (US) beat Ilie Nastase in the Men's Singles Final. It was his only Wimbledon title.
In the Women's Final, Billie Jean King (US) beat Yvonne Goolagong (AUS) to gain her fourth **Wimbledon** title.
The **Olympic Games** held in Munich are overshadowed by the murder of eleven Israeli athletes and coaches by Palestinian Black September members.

1973 George Foreman knocks out Joe Frazier in only two rounds to take the **World Heavyweight Boxing** Championship title.

Red Rum wins the **Grand National** with a new record and staging a spectacular comeback on the run-in having trailed the leader by 15 lengths at the final fence.

1974 Liverpool win the **FA Cup Final** against Newcastle United at Wembley. Kevin Keegan scored two of their three goals.
Eddie Merckx wins the **Tour de France**, becoming the first rider to win the Triple Crown of Cycling, **Tour de France**, **Giro d'Italia** and **World Championships** in one calendar year.

1975 - 1979

1975 In athletics, John Walker (NZ) sets a new world record becoming the first man to **run a mile** in under 3 mins 50 seconds. He clocks 3mins 49.4 secs.
Muhammad Ali defeats Joe Frazier in the 'Thrilla In Manilla' to maintain the **Boxing Heavyweight Championship** of the world.

1976 The **Olympics** are held in Montreal. Britain's only medal is a Bronze, won by Brendan Foster running the **10,000 metres**.
John Curry, becomes the **European, Olympic and World Figure Skating Champion**. He was the first skater to combine, ballet and modern dance into his skating.

1977 The commercial **World Series Cricket** was introduced by Kerry Packer. WSC changed the nature of the game with its emphasis on the "gladiatorial" aspect of fast bowling and heavy promotion of fast bowlers.

1978 During the **Oxford and Cambridge Boat Race,** the Cambridge boat sinks. It is the first sinking in the race since 1951.
Wales wins the rugby **Five Nations Championship** and completes the Grand Slam having beaten England, France, Ireland and Scotland.

1978 Arsenal beat Manchester United 3-2 in the **FA Cup Final.**
At **The Open** at Royal Lytham & St Annes Golf Club Seve Ballesteros becomes the first golfer from Continental Europe to win a major since 1907.

IN THE 1970s

Traffic Lights and Football

Before the introduction of Red and Yellow Cards in football, cautions or sending a player off had to be dealt with orally, and the language barrier could sometimes present problems. For example, in the 1966 World Cup, the German referee tried in vain to send Argentinian player Antonio Rattin off the field, but Rattin did not 'want' to understand and eventually was escorted off the pitch by the police! Ken Aston, Head of World Cup Referees, was tasked with solving this problem and legend has it that the idea of the red and yellow cards came to him when he was stopped in his car at traffic lights. They were tested in the 1968 Olympics and the 1970 World Cup in Mexico and introduced to European leagues soon after and after six years, to English football.

In 1976, the first player to be sent off using a red card in an English game was Blackburn Rovers winger David Wagstaffe.

Tour de France

In 1974 the Tour de France covered 2,546 miles in 22 stages, one of which was the first to be held in the UK, a circuit stage on the Plympton By-pass near Plymouth. Eddy Merckx of Belgium won eight stages and won the race overall with a comfortable margin, making it five wins for him out of his five Tours. He also won that year's Combination Classification – the General (Yellow Jersey), Points or Sprint (Green Jersey) and Mountains (since 1975, King of the Mountains wears the Polka Dot Jersey).

Rockstar and Racing Driver

James Hunt, the charismatic, play-boy darling of the press in the 1970's, began his Formula 1 career at the beginning of the decade with the Hesketh Racing team and gave them their only win in 1975 at the Dutch GP. He moved to McLaren in 1976, and in his first year with them, he and his great rival Niki Lauda at Ferrari, fought an epic season-long battle. It was an extraordinarily dramatic season, over sixteen races filled with drama and controversy, where Lauda had gained an early championship lead. By the final race in Japan, he was being reeled-in by Hunt and was only three points ahead. Hunt drove the race of his life, in the worst possible weather conditions, to finish in third place. Lauda, already badly injured from the crash at Nürburgring in August, withdrew because of the hazardous conditions which meant James Hunt became World Champion, winning by just a single point.

Hunt's natural driving ability was phenomenal, and while his habit of risk-taking didn't always endear him to others, hence the nickname "Hunt the Shunt", it also made him compelling to watch. Off track, he and Niki had an enduring friendship, which lasted after James's retirement from F1 in 1979 until his untimely death from a heart attack in 1993, aged just 45.

67

TRANSPORT

ICONIC MACHINES OF THE DECADE

The Jumbo Jet
Entered service on January 22, 1970. The 747 was the first airplane dubbed a "Jumbo Jet", the first wide-body airliner.

In 1971 Ford launched the car that was to represent the 1970s, the Cortina Mk III. In 1976 the Mk IV and 1979 Mk V. Cortinas were the best-selling cars of the decade.

The best-selling foreign import was the Datsun Sunny, which was only the 19th best-selling car of the decade.

In 1973, British Leyland's round, dumpy shaped Allegro was not at all popular and meagre sales contributed greatly to BL's collapse in 1975.

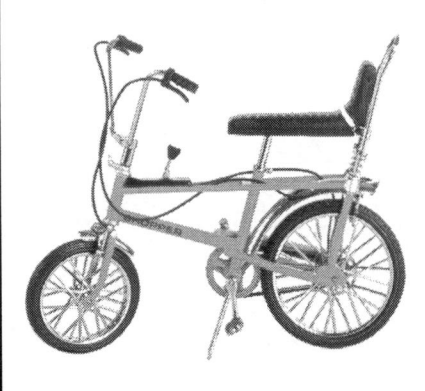

Raleigh Chopper
Shot to fame in the 70's when every child, and some adults, wanted one. It had a high back, long seat and motorbike rear wheel and was probably the first bike to have a centrally positioned gear shift.

"Sunblest Bread Lorry
Together with Mother's Pride, this was one of the iconic lorries of the '70's.

IN THE 1970s

Women Drivers

In 1974, Jill Viner became the first female bus driver for London Transport. She trained to become a bus driver at a centre in Chiswick in 1974, when London Transport were said to be 3,200 drivers short
While women had previously driven buses within bus depots during the Second World War, Viner was the first women to drive a bus in service in London. In the weeks after she started driving, it was reported that thirty women had applied to become bus drivers.

In 1978, Hannah Dadds completed a seven-week training course to qualify as a train driver and became the first female driver on the London Underground.
Hannah's sister Edna also joined the London Underground working first as a guard and then a driver. Hannah and Edna became the first all-female crew on the London Underground.

Concorde

The Anglo-French supersonic passenger airliner had a take-off speed of 220 knots (250mph) and a cruising speed of 1350mph – more than twice the speed of sound. With seating for 92 to 128 passengers, Concorde entered service in 1976 and operated for 27 years.
Twenty aircraft were built in total, including six prototypes and in the end, only Air France and British Airways purchased and flew them, due in great part to supersonic flights being restricted to ocean-crossing routes, to prevent sonic boom disturbance over land and populated areas. Concorde flew regular transatlantic flights from London and Paris to New York, Washington, Dulles in Virginia and Barbados and the BA Concorde made just under 50,000 flights and flew more than 2.5m passengers supersonically.

A typical London to New York crossing would take a little less than three and a half hours as opposed to about eight hours for a subsonic flight.

The aircraft was retired in 2003, three years after the crash of an Air France flight in which all passengers and crew were killed.

THE MAJOR NEWS STORIES

1980 - 1984

1980:

May: Mount St. Helens experiences a huge eruption that creates avalanches, explosions, large ash clouds, mudslides, and massive damage. 57 people are killed.

Dec: John Lennon, the former Beatle, age 40, is shot and killed by an obsessed fan in Manhattan.

1981:

July: Prince Charles marries Lady Diana Spencer at St Paul's Cathedral.

Margaret Thatcher's Government begins the privatisation of the Nationalised Industries.

1982:

Apr: Argentina invades the Falkland Islands and the UK retakes possession of them by the end of June.

May: Pope John Paul II visits the United Kingdom. It is the first visit by a reigning Pope

1983:

Apr: The £1 coin is introduced in the UK.

Jun: Margaret Thatcher wins a landslide victory for the Conservatives in the General Election, with a majority of 144.

Nov: The first United States cruise missiles arrive at RAF Greenham Common in Berkshire

1984:

Mar: The National Mineworkers Union led by Arthur Scargill, begin what will be a year-long strike against the National Coal Board's plans to shut 20 collieries

May: The Thames Barrier, designed to protect London from floods, is opened by The Queen

1980: Mount St. Helens before and after the eruption. The top third of the mountain was blown away.

1982: EPCOT opened at Disney World in Florida, "...an experimental prototype community of tomorrow that will take its cue from the new ideas and technologies that are now emerging ... a showcase of the ingenuity and imagination of American free enterprise." - *Walt Disney*

1984: On 31 October, Indira Gandhi, Prime Minister of India, was killed by her Sikh bodyguards.
The assassination sparked four days of riots that left more than 8,000 Indian Sikhs dead in revenge attacks.

OF THE 1980s

1985 - 1989

1985:
Jan: The Internet's Domain Name System is created and the country code top-level domain .uk is registered in July.

Dec: The original charity "Comic Relief" is launched by Richard Curtis and Lenny Henry on Christmas Day,.

1986:
Apr: A Soviet Nuclear reactor at Chernobyl explodes causing the release of radioactive material across much of Europe.

Oct: The 'Big Bang' – the London Stock Exchange is deregulated allowing computerised share dealing.

1987:
Jan: Terry Waite, the special envoy of the Archbishop of Canterbury in Lebanon, is kidnapped in Beirut. He is held in captivity for 1,763 days until 1991.

Oct: Black Monday: Wall Street crash leads to £50,000,000,000 being wiped of the value of shares on the London stock exchange.

1988:
Dec: Suspected Libyan terrorist bomb explodes on Pan Am jet over Lockerbie in Scotland on December 21st killing all 259 on board and 11 on the ground.

Dec: Health Minister Edwina Currie states that most of Britain's egg production is infected with salmonella, causing an immediate nationwide slump in egg sales.

1989:
Apr: 94 fans are killed in the Hillsborough football stadium collapse in Sheffield. 3 more will die and over 300 are hospitalised.

Nov: The Fall of the Berlin Wall heralds the end of the Cold War and communism in East and Central Europe.

1985: On 1st January, Ernie Wise made the first, civilian, mobile phone call in the UK from outside the Dicken's Inn at St Katharine's Dock. Via the Vodafone network he called their office in Newbury on a VT1 which weighed 5.5kg.

1987: Oct 15th: Weather-man Michael Fish: "Earlier on today, a woman rang the BBC and said she heard there was a hurricane on the way... well, if you're watching, don't worry, there isn't!". That night, hurricane force winds hit much of the South of England killing 23 people, bringing down an estimated 15 million trees and causing damage estimated at £7.3 billion.

THE HOME

A Busier Life

In the 1980's, life became more stressful, there were two recessions, divorce rates were increasing, women were exercising their rights and these years were the beginning of the end of the traditional family unit. With single parent families or both parents at work and a generally 'busier' life, there was a fundamental change to the family and home. There was also a lot more choice.

Many more 'lower cost' restaurants, chilled ready-made meals, instant foods such as Findus Crispy Pancakes, Pot Noodles or M&S Chicken Kievs and the, by now, ubiquitous tea bag, together with the consumer boom in electrical labour-saving devices from food processors and microwaves to automatic washing machines, dishwashers and sandwich toasters and jug kettles, all added up to more free time from housework and cooking.

Floral Décor

Flower patterns were all the rage in early 1980s home décor, with flower patterned upholstery and curtains to floral wallpapers taking over from the 70s woodchip paper.

Artex was still hugely popular on ceilings and walls, finished with the familiar stippled or swirled patterns and peach was *the* fashionable colour of choice for interior design schemes. Chintz curtains could have more layers, swags and tails than an onion! The bold reached the height of fashion with a red and black colour scheme, black ash furniture and a framed Ferrari print on the wall – with a bold wallpaper border at the ceiling which often clashed with the paper on the walls.

IN THE 1980s

The Telephone Answering Machine

There once was a time when, to use a telephone, both people had to be on the phone at the same time. You had to pick up the phone when it rang. The answering machine, one cassette tape for the outgoing message and one to record incoming calls, changed all that. By allowing people to take calls when they were away and respond to any message at a later time.

Children's Playtime

For children, toys of the early 80s had a bit of a 70s feel, Star Wars action figures, remote controlled cars and trucks, Barbie dolls and Action Men, but by 1983 there was a huge increase in toys like Transformers, Care Bears, a plethora of talking robot toys, My Little Pony, Teenage Mutant Ninja Turtles and Cabbage Patch Kids which was THE craze of 1983 – these odd looking 'little people' were the first images to feature on disposable 'designer' nappies!

Basic Atari video games evolved to Nintendo's NES game system and all of them competed with Apple and Sinclair home computers and personal Walkman stereos.

Art and Culture

1980 - 1984

1980 "Who shot J.R.?" was an advertising catchphrase that CBS created to promote their TV show, 'Dallas', referring to the cliff hanger of the finale of the previous season. The episode, 'Who Done It?' aired in November with an estimated 83 million viewers tuning in.

MV Mi Amigo, the ship 'Radio Caroline', the pirate radio station, operates from, runs aground and sinks off Sheerness.

1981 A bronze statue of Charlie Chaplin, as his best loved character, The Tramp, is unveiled in Leicester Square.

1982 The D'Oyly Carte Opera Company gives its last performance at the end of a final London season, having been in near-continuous existence since 1875.

1983 Children's ITV is launched in Britain as a new branding for the late afternoon programming block on the ITV network.

1984 The comedian Tommy Cooper collapses and dies on stage from a heart attack during a live televised show, 'Live from Her Majesty's'.

Ted Hughes is appointed Poet Laureate and succeeds Sir John Betjeman. Philip Larkin had turned down the post.

1985 - 1989

1985 The Roux Brothers' Waterside Inn at Bray, Berkshire becomes the first establishment in the UK to be awarded three Michelin stars.

'Live Aid' pop concerts in London and Philadelphia raise over £50,000,000 for famine relief in Ethiopia.

1986 The Sun newspaper alleges that comedian Freddie Starr ate a live hamster.

More than 30m viewers watched the Christmas Day episode of 'East Enders' in which Den Watts serves the divorce papers on his wife Angie.

1987 Christie's auction house in London sells one of Vincent van Gogh's iconic Sunflowers paintings for £24,750,000 after a bidding war between two unidentified competitors bidding via telephone.

'The Simpsons' cartoon first appears as a series of animated short films on the 'Tracey Ullman Show' in the US.

1988 Salman Rushdie published 'The Satanic Verses' a work of fiction which caused a widespread furore and forced Rushdie to live in hiding out of fear for his life.

1989 Sky Television begins broadcasting as the first satellite TV service in Britain.

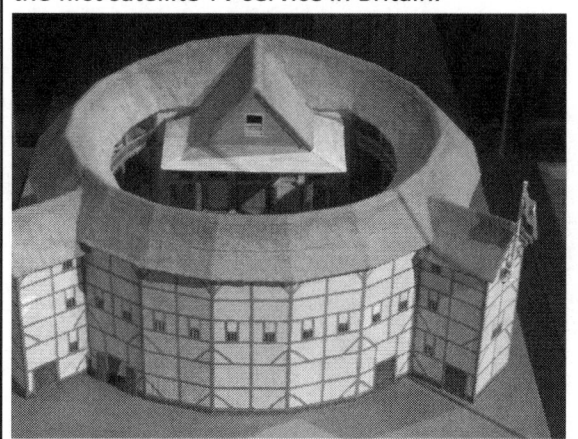

Remains of both The Rose, an Elizabethan playhouse, and the Globe Theatre are found in London.

IN THE 1980s

The Great Musical Revival

By the start of the 1980's, Britain was in recession and the West End Theatres were facing rising costs and falling audiences – until the revival of the Musical, led by Andrew Lloyd Webber.

In 1981, his first 'unlikely' musical **Cats** led by Elaine Paige, went on to be the first 'megamusical' spectacular in the West End and on Broadway.

It was followed in 1984 by **Starlight Express.**

By now, these shows were being enjoyed not only by home audiences but also, a massive 44% of tickets, were purchased by tourists.

In 1986, the **Phantom of the Opera** opened to overwhelmingly positive reviews.

In 1987 **Les Misérables** brought the Royal Shakespeare Company's expertise in high drama to the musical which was set amidst the French Revolution and brought fame to its writers, Alain Boubill and Claude-Michel Schönberg fame and producer Cameron Mackintosh his millions.

Other hit musicals of the decade: Willy Russel's **Blood Brothers**, Noël Gay's revival of **Me and My Girl**, and Lloyd Webber's **Aspects of Love.**

Films

1980 - 1984

1980 The epic **The Empire Strikes Back** is released and is the highest-grossing film of the year, just as its predecessor, **Star Wars** was in 1977. However, the Oscar for Best Picture went to **Ordinary People**, the psychological drama depicting the disintegration of an upper middle-class family in Illinois.

1981 Chariots of Fire based on the true story of two British athletes, one Christian, one Jewish in the 1924 Olympics, won the Academy Awards.
The film's title was inspired by the line "Bring me my Chariot of fire!" from Blake's poem adapted as the hymn 'Jerusalem'.

1982 Spielberg's science fiction film of **ET the Extra Terrestrial** was a huge box office hit this year, the scene when the little green extra-terrestrial learns to speak, instilled "ET phone home" into the collective memory. The rather more down to earth biographical film of Mahatma Gandhi **Gandhi**, picked up the Best Film award.

1983 There were many great British films this year including **Local Hero** and **Educating Rita, The Dresser** and Sean Connery playing Bond for the last time in **Never Say Never Again.** It was the American, **Terms of Endearment** that won the Oscars.

1984 Amadeus the fictionalised story of the composer Wolfgang Amadeus Mozart and a supposed rivalry with Italian composer Antonio Salieri, featuring much of Mozart's music, won the imagination of the audiences and the Best Film of the Year award too.

1985 - 1989

1985 Spielberg's 'coming of age' epic starring Whoopi Goldberg in her breakthrough role, **The Color Purple**, was nominated for eleven Academy Awards but failed to achieve a single win. The prize went to Meryl Streep and Robert Redford in the romantic drama, **Out of Africa.**

1986 The first of Oliver Stone's trilogy based on his experiences in the Vietnam war, **Platoon** picks up this year's Oscar for Best Film, beating two British nominations, **A Room with a View** and **The Mission**. This was also the year of the Australian box office runaway success, **Crocodile Dundee.**

1987 The thriller **Fatal Attraction** attracted both favourable reviews and controversy. It put the phrase 'bunny boiler' into the urban dictionary.

1988 Glenn Close was nominated for Best Actress for her role as the Marquise de Merteuil who plots revenge against her ex-lover, in **Dangerous Liaisons**. Dustin Hoffman and Tom Cruise starred in **Rainman**, the winner of Best Film of the year.

1989 Unusually, it was a PG rated film, **Driving Miss Daisy** that won the Academy Award this year, a gentle, heartwarming comedy which had the serious themes of racism and anti-semitism at its heart. Jessica Tandy at age 81, won Best Actress, the oldest winner to do so.

In The 1980s

David Puttnam, Baron Puttnam of Queensgate (1997)

The 1980s saw the release of several films by the British producer, David Puttnam, beginning with, in 1981, his most successful film up until that time, **Chariots of Fire**.

His next big success was **Local Hero** the comedy drama, set on the west coast of Scotland where an American oil company wishes to purchase a local village and surrounding area.

Next, in 1984, came the acclaimed **Cal**, a young man on the fringes of the IRA who falls in love with a Catholic woman whose husband, a Protestant policeman, had been killed by the IRA one year earlier. Entered into the Cannes Film Festival, Helen Mirren won Best Actress.

Also in 1984, Puttnam produced **The Killing Fields**, a harrowing biographical drama about the Khmer Rouge in Cambodia, based on the experiences of a Cambodian journalist and an American journalist. This film received seven Oscar nominations and won three, most notably Best Supporting Actor for Haing S. Ngor who had no previous acting experience.

Puttnam's career spanned the 1960s to the 1990s and his films have won 10 Oscars, 31 BAFTAs, 13 Golden Globes, nine Emmys, four David di Donatellos in Italy and the Palme d'Or at Cannes.

FASHION

A Fashion Statement

The mid to late 80s was the time to 'make a statement'. The mass media took over fashion trends completely and fashion magazines, TV shows and music videos all played a part in dictating the latest bold fashions.

There was a huge emphasis on bright colours, huge shoulder pads, power suits which gave an exaggerated silhouette like an upside-down triangle, flashy skirts and spandex leggings, velour, leg warmers and voluminous parachute pants.

We wore iconic oversized plastic hoop earrings, rubber bracelets and shiny chain necklaces and huge sunglasses giving faces the appearance of large flies. Men and women alike made their hair 'big' with or without the ubiquitous teased perm and for the girls, glossy pink lips, overly filled-in brows, rainbow-coloured eyeshadows and exaggerated blusher were on trend.

Men too joined in with style and sported oversized blazers with shiny buttons, pinstripe two-piece suits and sweaters, preferably from Ralph Lauren, draped over the shoulders.

Polka Dots

Although not new to the 80s - Disney's Minnie Mouse was first seen in the 1920's wearing the red and white dottie print - polka dots were also very popular.

Bands such as The Beat used them in their music videos and well-known celebrities including Madonna and Princess Diana loved the cool look of polka dot dresses and tops.

When teamed with the oversized earrings of the decade and big hair, whilst bucking the trend for bright, gaudy colours, they still "made a statement".

Carolina Herrera used polka dots on most of her dresses during the late 1980s and early 1990s and it remains a key print in her collections, a classic.

As Marc Jacobs, the American designer famously said, "There is never a wrong time for a polka dot."

IN THE 1980s

Labels, logos and idols

Pale blue, distressed jeans were the fashionable 'street wear', worn semi fitted and held with a statement belt at the natural waistline. When the boy band Bros came along in 1988, wearing jeans ripped at the knee coupled with leather, slip on loafers, teens up and down the country enthusiastically took the scissors to their own jeans, and ripped, frayed or shredded them.

Pop Fashion

If you were into pop music in the 1980s, there's no doubt that superstar Madonna influenced what you wore.

Feet also presented a branding opportunity, Patrick Cox had celebrities make his loafers universally desired, and, often credited with kicking off the whole fashion sneaker movement, Nike Air 'Jordans' – named after basketball star, Michael Jordan – were launched in 1985. If you couldn't have them, then high-top Reebok sneakers were also the pinnacle of style -- as were Adidas Superstar kicks and matching tracksuits.

LEISURE

The Fitness Craze

The 1980's had a fitness craze. Celebrities made aerobics videos and endorsed weight loss products and equipment. Health Clubs and Gyms became the place to be and to be seen but were predominantly for men so for women who wanted to exercise in the privacy of their own home, by the mid '80s, there were very few households that didn't own at least one well-worn VHS copy of **'Jane Fonda's Workout'**.

Her 1982 video sold more than 17 million copies, with the actress wearing a striped and belted leotard, violet leggings and leg warmers, big, big hair and in full make-up and working up a sweat to some heavy synth music, inspired a whole generation.

At home, between 1983 and 1987, Britain's answer to Jane Fonda, Diana Moran **'The Green Goddess'**, appeared on TV screens wearing her trade-mark green leotard telling millions of BBC Breakfast viewers to 'wake up and shape up' with her aerobics routines.

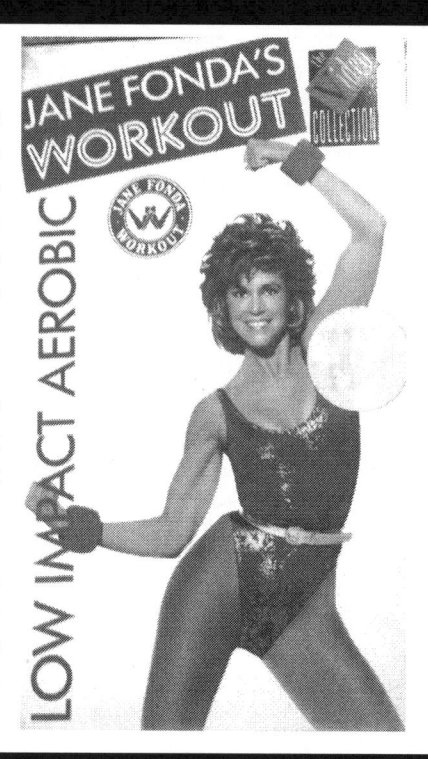

What's On Telly?

Television was a very large part of leisure in the 1980s and with the massive growth in video recorders, the whole family had more control over what they watched and when they watched it.

It was the decade when the huge American 'soaps' **Dallas** and **Dynasty** dominated the ratings and influenced popular debate as well as fashions. In Britain there was a rash of police dramas and the introduction of female detectives in both BBC **'Juliet Bravo'** and ITV **'The Gentle Touch'**. They also covered the land, **'Taggart'** in Scotland, **'Bergerac'** in Jersey, **'The Chinese Detective'** in London and **'Inspector Morse'** in Oxford.

Channel 4 launched in 1982 with its first programme being **'Countdown'**, Breakfast TV began in 1983, in 1980s television produced 'historic' shared experiences, **'Who Shot JR'** in Dallas watched by 80 million, the finale of **MASH**, 'Goodbye, Farewell and Amen', by more than 100 million, 30 million tuned in to watch 'Dirty Den' serve his wife 'Angie' with the divorce papers in East Enders and 27 million watched the episode after Alan Bradley tried to kill Rita Fairclough in **Coronation Street.**

IN THE 1980s

What Was New?

Whilst the 80s made huge advances in technology for leisure, Game Boy and Nintendo, VCRs and CDs, disposable cameras and brick shaped mobile phones too, there were other innovations.

In the 'yuppie' years of 'spend, spend, spend', the first smart chip-enabled credit cards were busy being swiped for BMX bikes, Trivial Pursuit and Rubik's Cubes.

Nike told us to 'Just Do It' and we wondered how we'd ever managed without Post-It Notes and disposable contact lenses.

What the world did not want however, was New Coke. Coca Cola changed their classic formula for a sweeter one which received an extremely poor response.

It was one of the worst marketing blunders ever because for the public, this tampered recipe 'Just wasn't it!'. The company brought back the original Coke and sold this new formula as the 'New Coke' till the early 90s.

Music

1980 - 1984

1980 Johnny Logan won the Eurovision Song Contest for Ireland with **What's Another Year** and was No 1 in the UK charts for two weeks in May. He won again in 1987 with **Hold Me Now**.
Abba had their first No 1 of the year with **Winner Takes it All** followed in November with **Super Trouper.**

1981 Two singles stayed at the top of the charts for 5 weeks each this year. First Adam and the Ants with **Stand and Deliver** and in December, The Human League with **Don't You Want Me** which was also the best-selling single of the year.

1982 The year's best seller was Dexey's Midnight Runners and **Come on Eileen**, their second No 1 in the UK. The words express the feelings of an adolescent dreaming of being free from the strictures of a Catholic society and sounded unlike the other hits of the era, no synthesiser, but a banjo, accordion, fiddle and saxophone.

1983 **Karma Chameleon** by the 'New Romantic' band, Culture Club, fronted by singer Boy George, whose androgynous style of dressing caught the attention of the public and the media, became the second Culture Club single to reach No 1 and stayed there for six weeks, also becoming the best-selling single of the year.

1984 Two Tribes, the anti-war song by the Liverpool band, Frankie Goes to Hollywood, was a phenomenal success helped by a wide range of remixes and supported by an advertising campaign depicting the band as members of the Red Army. It entered the charts at No 1 and stayed there for nine consecutive weeks, making it the the longest-running No 1 single of the decade.

1985 - 1989

1985 The best seller this year was **The Power of Love** sung by Jennifer Rush. No 1 for five weeks, Rush became the first female artist ever to have a million-selling single in the UK.
Wham and George Michael, having had three No 1's last year, **Wake Me Up Before You Go-Go, Careless Whisper** and **Freedom**, managed only one this year, **I'm Your Man.**

1986 Holiday disco songs such as **Agadoo**, topped the charts for three weeks.
The Christmas No 1 spot was held for four weeks by a reissue, three years after his death, of Jackie Wilson's **Reet Petite (The Sweetest Girl in Town)**.

1987 Two singles stayed at No 1 for five weeks, the best-selling of the year, **Never Gonna Give You Up** by Rick Astley and **China in Your Hand** by T'Pau, Carol Decker's group named after the character in Star Trek.

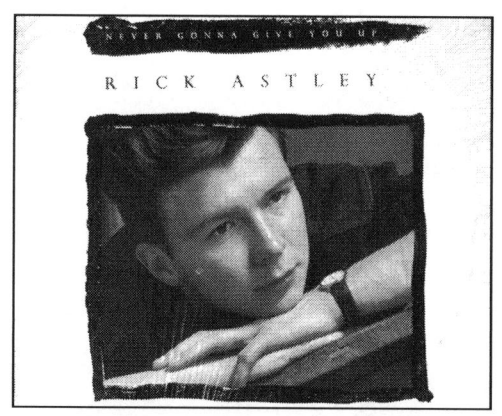

1988 Already known from the Australian soap opera, 'Neighbours', Kylie Minogue burst into the UK charts with **I Should Be So Lucky** from her debut studio album. The song became a worldwide hit.
Cliff Richard was back at No 1 after quite a break, with **Mistletoe and Wine** for the Christmas market.

1989 It was a good year for the Australian golden couple, Jason Donovan and Kylie Minogue. One No 1 together, **Especially For You,** two for Jason, **Too Many Broken Hearts** and **Sealed With a Kiss**, and one for Kylie, **Hand on Your Heart.**
Ride on Time from the debut album by Italian house music group, Black Box, topped the charts for six weeks and sold the most copies of the year.

IN THE 1980s

Charity Fund Raisers

The 80's saw many 'not for profit' Charity Singles, the best-known being Bob Geldorf and Midge Ure's 'Band Aid' and then 'Live Aid', formed to raise money for famine relief in Ethiopia, who released **Do They Know Its Christmas**, for the first time, in December 1984. It stayed at the top of the charts for five weeks and was the best-selling record of the decade having been released again in 1989.

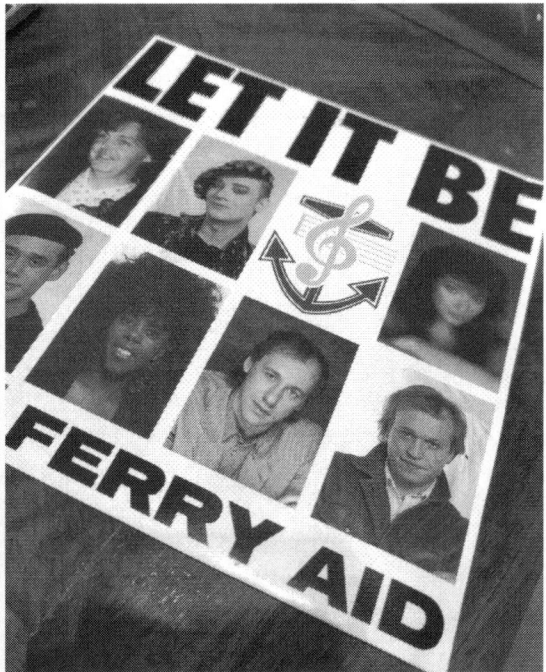

A less well-known charity, 'Ferry Aid', recorded the Beatles' song, **Let It Be** in 1987. This followed the sinking of the ferry 'Ms Herald of the Free' at Zeebrugge, killing 193 passengers and crew. The recording was organised by The Sun newspaper, after it had sold cheap tickets for the ferry on that day.

Tears For Fears, Duran Duran and Simple Minds got together and released **Everybody Wants to Rule the World** in 1986 in support of 'Sport Aid', a campaign to help tackle famine in Africa.

In 1983, Michael Jackson redefined the style, course, and possibilities of music videos. He released **Thriller** and made recording history. The album spent thirty-seven weeks at No 1 on the US Billboard chart. By early 1984, thirty million copies had been sold, and it was still selling at a rate of more than a million copies a week worldwide.

SCIENCE AND NATURE

The Compact Disc

In 1981, Kieran Prendiville on BBC's 'Tomorrow's World', demonstrated the CD and wondered, "Whether or not there is a market for these discs, remains to be seen." Well, on the 25th anniversary of its first public release in 1982, it was estimated that 200 billion CDs had been sold worldwide so I guess the answer was "Yes"!

At the end of the 70's, Philips and Sony had teamed up to begin working on CDs for the public and decided on a thin, shiny and circular storage disc, which could hold about 80 minutes of music. The disc had a diameter of 120mm, Sony having insisted that the longest musical performance, Beethoven's entire 9th Symphony at 74 minutes, should fit. A CD could hold an immense amount of data, much more than the vinyl record or the cassette and was perfectly portable.

The first commercial CD to be pressed was **Visitors** by Abba, followed quickly by the first album, Billy Joel's **52nd Street**. The biggest selling CD of all time is the Eagles 1976 **Their Greatest Hits** album, which has sold over 38 million copies.

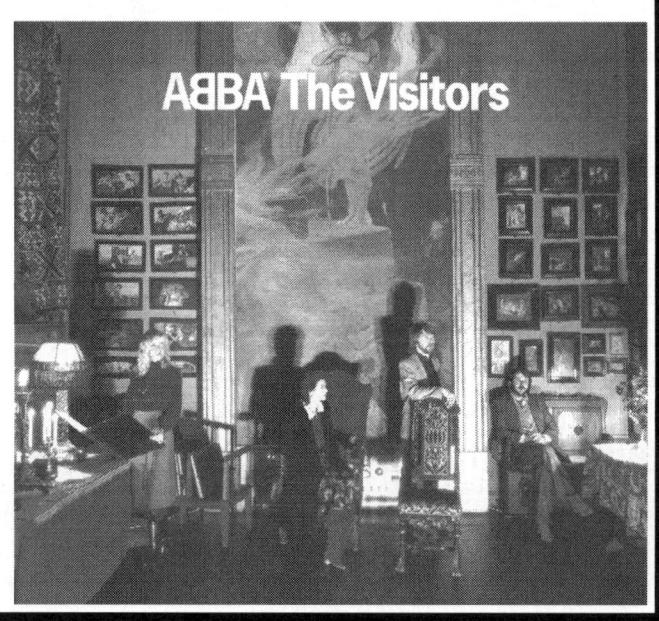

UFOs in the Forest

On 26 December 1980, several US Airforce personnel stationed near the east gate at RAF Woodbridge, reported they had seen "lights" apparently descending into nearby Rendlesham Forest. They initially thought it was a downed aircraft but, upon investigation, they saw what they described as a glowing object, metallic in appearance, with coloured lights.

After daybreak on the morning of December 27, servicemen returned to a small clearing in the forest and found three small impressions on the ground in a triangular pattern, as well as burn marks and broken branches on nearby trees.

The 'Rendlesham Forest Incident' made headline news and theories suggest it was either an actual alien visitation, a secret military aircraft, a misinterpretation of natural lights, the beam of Orfordness Lighthouse, or just a hoax.

IN THE 1980s

Mount St Helens

In March 1980 a series of volcanic explosions began at Mount St Helens, Washington in the US, culminating in a major explosive eruption on May 18. The eruption column rose 80,000 feet (15 miles) into the atmosphere and deposited ash over 11 states and into some Canadian provinces. At the same time, snow, ice, and entire glaciers on the volcano melted, forming a series of large volcanic mudslides that reached as far as 50 miles to the southwest. Thermal energy released during the eruption was equal to 26 megatons of TNT.

Regarded as the most significant and disastrous volcanic eruption in the country's history, about 57 people were killed, hundreds of square miles were reduced to wasteland, thousands of animals were killed, and Mount St. Helens was left with a crater on its north side. The area is now preserved as the Mount St Helens National Volcanic Monument.

One day before the eruption and several months afterwards. About a third of the mountain was blown away.

SPORT

1980 - 1984

1980 Eight days after the **Boston marathon**, Rosie Ruiz, a Cuban American, is disqualified as the winner 'in the fastest time ever run by a woman'. Investigations found that she did not run the entire course, joining about a half-mile before the finish.

Larry Holmes defeats Muhammed Ali to retain boxing's **WBC World Heavyweight** title. It is Ali's last world title bout.

1981 At **Wimbledon**, John McEnroe defeats Björn Borg to gain his 3rd career Grand Slam title and his 1st Wimbledon title.
In the ladies' final, Chris Evert Lloyd defeats Hana Mandlíková to gain her 12th career Grand Slam title and her third and last Wimbledon title.

1982 In June, at Pebble Beach, the American Tom Watson wins **The US Open** and a month later, at Royal Troon, he wins the **The Open.** He is only the third golfer, at that time, to win both Championships in the same year.
In Spain, Italy defeat West Germany in the **World Cup Final.** The tournament features the first penalty shoot-out in the World Cup competition.

1983 The **FA Cup** is won by Manchester United who, having drawn the first final with Brighton and Hove Albion, win the replay, 4-0.

1984 John McEnroe has his best season. He wins 13 singles tournaments, including **Wimbledon** where he loses just one set on his way to his third Wimbledon singles title. This includes a straight set win over Jimmy Connors in the final. He also wins the **US Open**, capturing the year-end number one ranking.

1985 - 1989

1985 Ireland is the championship winner in the **Rugby Five Nations** winning their tenth solo title, but it would prove to be their last for 24 years, until their Grand Slam in 2009.
Alain Prost becomes the **F1 World Champion** Driver, winning five of the sixteen Grand Prix. The first ever world championship **Australian Grand Prix** is held on a street circuit in Adelaide.

1986 In the **World Cup**, Argentina wins by defeating West Germany 3-2. Diego Maradona is the biggest star of the event, and his 'Hand of God' goal is well remembered. The event also sees the introduction of the 'Mexican Wave'.

1987 In **Cricket** the Indian opening batsman, Sunil Gavaskar reaches 10,000 test runs to become the first ever player to score this many. In the **Cricket World Cup** played for the first time outside Britain, in India, Australia win by defeating their arch-rivals, England.

1988 The **FA Cup** is won by Wimbledon FC's 'Crazy Gang', who defeat league champions Liverpool through a headed goal by Lawrie Sanchez. This is Wimbledon's only FA Cup title during its lifetime.

1989 On heavy, almost un-raceable ground, the iconic grey Desert Orchid, ridden by Simon Sherwood, in a race that defined his illustrious career, wins the **Cheltenham Gold Cup**. In 2005 this was voted the 'Greatest Race of All Time' by Racing Post readers.

IN THE 1980s

You cannot be serious!

During the 1981 Wimbledon Championships, John McEnroe uttered what has become the most immortal phrase in tennis, if not all sport, when he screamed "you cannot be serious" at a Wimbledon umpire while disputing a line call. Already called "Superbrat" by the British tabloid press for his verbal volleys during previous Wimbledon matches, it was in a first-round match against fellow American Tom Gullikson, who was serving at 15-30 and 1-1 in the first set when a McEnroe shot was called out. Approaching the umpire, he said: "Chalk came up all over the place, you can't be serious man." Then, his anger rising, he bawled the words that would stay with him for a lifetime and find its way into the sporting annals. "You cannot be serious," he screamed. "That ball was on the line".

On the receiving end of the tirade was umpire Edward James, who eventually responded by politely announcing: "I'm going to award a point against you Mr McEnroe." It made little difference, McEnroe went on to win in straight sets and two weeks later had his final victory over Bjorn Borg.

Torvill and Dean

On Valentine's Day 1984, Jayne Torvill and Christopher Dean made history at the Winter Olympics in Sarajevo and set a new standard for world class figure skating. The duo from Nottingham, were the last to perform in their category and their performance, self-choreographed to 4½ minutes of Ravel's Bolero, was seamless, elegant and hypnotic. As they sank to the ice in the dramatic finale, the whole stadium stood and applauded. Their dance had captured the world's imagination and won Gold. The unanimous scores of 6.0 for artistic impression made them the highest-scoring figure skaters of all time.

Their routine, made Ravel's Boléro with its steady crescendo and repeated snare-drum rhythms, synonymous with figure-skating.

Transport

British Car Manufacturing

Gallery:
The 1980s was still a busy period for British car manufacturers and many of the bestselling cars of the decade were made in Britain.
The top 10 cars were:
1. Ford Escort
2. Vauxhall Cavalier
3. Ford Fiesta
4. Austin Metro
5. Ford Sierra (which replaced the
6. Ford Cortina)
6. Vauxhall Astra
7. Ford Orion
8. Austin Maestro
9. Vauxhall Nova
10. Ford Grenada

However the list of the **'Most influential Cars of the 1980s'** shows how the British car industry was soon to be decimated. The list includes:
Audi Quatrro; Porsche 944: Renault Scenic; Mercedes 190; BMW 3 Series; VW Golf; Volvo 240 Estate; Peugeot 205 and the Toyota Carolla.

The Ford Cortina was replaced by the Ford Sierra in 1982

The Ford Fiesta has been ever popular right up to the present day.

The Austin Metro was the replacement for the mini.

The VW Golf had front wheel drive and built a reputation for quality and reliability

The Porsche 944 was the choice of the newly rich 'yuppies' of the 1980s

Clunk Click Every Trip

Although car manufacturers had been obliged to install seatbelts since 1965, it was not until January 1983 that the law requiring all drivers to wear their belts came into force. In spite of a great deal of 'grumbling' and more, ranging from *"the erosion of our civil liberties, another example of the Nanny State"*, to *"its uncomfortable, restrictive and creases my clothes"* and horror stories of crash victims being *"hanged"* by their belts or suffering greater injury, 90% of drivers and front seat passengers were observed to be wearing seat belts soon after the law came into effect – and these rates have been sustained since then. There was an immediate 25% reduction in driver fatalities and a 29 per cent reduction in fatal injuries among front seat passengers.

In 1989 it became compulsory for all children under 14 to wear a seat belt in the rear and when seatbelt wearing became compulsory for all rear-seat occupants in 1991, there was an immediate increase from 10% to 40% in observed seat belt wearing rates.

In The 1980s

Aviation

When Airbus designed the A300 during the late 1960s and early 1970s, it envisaged a broad family of airliners with which to compete against Boeing and Douglas, the two established US aerospace manufacturers.

The launch of the A320 in 1987 guaranteed the status of Airbus as a major player in the aircraft market – the aircraft had over 400 orders before it first flew.

Motorcycles

Only 3000 Honda FVR750R motorcycles were made, race bred machines with lights thrown on to make them road legal and sold to the public. The first batch of 1000 sold out instantly. With a top speed of 153mph the V-four powered RC30 was one of the fastest sports bike of the decade but it was the track proven frame that meant it handled like a genuine racer. It also had a soundtrack to die for and was absolutely beautiful.

The Docklands Light Railway

The Docklands Light Railway was first opened in August 1987 as an automated, light metro system to serve the redeveloped Docklands area of London as a cheap public transport solution. The original network comprised two routes - Tower Gateway to Island Gardens and Stratford to Island Gardens and was mainly elevated on disused railway viaducts, new concrete viaducts and disused surface railway tracks. The trains were fully automated, controlled by computer, and had no driver.

They did however have a "Train Captain" who was responsible for patrolling the train, checking tickets, making announcements and controlling the doors. They could take control of the train should there be an equipment failure or emergency. The first generation of rolling stock comprised eleven lightweight units and the stations, mostly of a common design, constructed from standard components and usually featuring a short half-cylindrical, glazed, blue canopy, were designed specifically for these single articulated trains. The 15 stations were all above ground and needed no staff.

THE MAJOR NEWS STORIES

1990 - 1994

1990:
Feb: Nelson Mandela is released from prison in South Africa, after 27 years behind bars.

Nov: Margaret Thatcher resigns as Prime Minister. At 11 years, she was the longest serving PM of the 20th Century.

1991:
Jan: The Gulf War begins, as the Royal Air Force joins Allied aircraft in bombing raids on Iraq

Apr: After a year of protests and riots, the government confirms that the Poll Tax is to be replaced by a new Council Tax in 1993.

1992:
Apr: At the General Election the Conservative Party are re-elected for a fourth term under John Major.

Nov: Part of Windsor Castle is gutted in a fire causing millions of pounds worth of damage and The Queen describes this year as an Annus Horribilis.

1993:
Apr: The Queen announces that Buckingham Palace will open to the public for the first time

Sep: The UK Independence Party which supports the breakaway from the EU is formed.

Dec: Diana, Princess of Wales. withdraws from public life.

1994:
Mar: The Church of England ordains its first female priests.

May: The Channel Tunnel between Britain and France is officially opened.

Nov: The first UK National Lottery draw takes place.

1992: The 'Maastricht Treaty' was concluded between the 'then' twelve member states of the European Communities. This foundation treaty of the EU announced a new stage in the process of European integration, shared citizenship and a single currency. There were two headquarters, one in Brussels and one in Strasbourg,

1991: The internet already existed but no one had thought of a way of how to link one document directly to another until in 1989, British scientist Tim Berners-Lee, invented the WorldWideWeb. The www. was introduced in 1991 as the first web browser and the first website went online in August.

Of The 1990s

1995 - 1999

1995:
Feb: Barings Bank, the UK's oldest merchant bank, collapses after rogue trader Nick Leeson loses $1.4 billion.

Apr: All telephone area dialling codes are changed in the UK.

Aug: Pubs in England are permitted to remain open throughout Sunday afternoon.

1996:
Feb: The Prince and Princess of Wales agree to divorce more than three years after separating.

Jul: Dolly the Sheep becomes the first mammal to be successfully cloned from an adult cell.

1997:
May: Tony Blair wins a landslide General Election for the Labour Party.

Aug: Princess Diana is killed in a car crash in Paris. Dodi Fayed, the heir to the Harrods empire is killed with her

1998:
Mar: Construction on the Millenium Dome begins. It will be the centre piece for a national celebration.

Apr: The Good Friday Agreement between the UK and Irish governments is signed.

1999:
Apr: A minimum wage is introduced in the UK – set at £3.60 an hour for workers over 21, and £3 for workers under 21

Jun: Construction of the Millenium Dome is finished and in October, the London Eye begins to be lifted into position.

1997: The UK transfers sovereignty of Hong Kong, the largest remaining British colony, to the People's Republic of China as the 99 years lease on the territory formally ends.

1999: On 1st January, the new European currency, the Euro is launched and some 320 million people from eleven European countries begin carrying the same money in their wallets.
Britain's Labour government preferred to stay with the pound sterling instead.

THE HOME

Home life in the 1990s was changing again. Family time was not cherished as it had once been, children had a lot more choice and were becoming more independent with their own TVs programmes, personal computers, music systems, mobile phones and, crucially, the introduction of the world wide web, which meant life would never be the same again.

After school and weekend organised activities for the young burgeoned, with teenagers able to take advantage of the fast-food chains, or eating at different times, meaning no more family eating together. Families 'lived in separate' rooms, there were often two televisions so different channels could be watched and children wanted to play with their Nintendos or listen to their Walkmans in their own rooms. Their rooms were increasingly themed, from Toy Story to Athena posters, a ceiling full of sticker stars that illuminated a room with their green glow and somewhere in the house, room had to be made for the computer desk.

Track lighting was an easy way to illuminate a room without relying on multiple lamps and it became a popular feature in many '90s homes along with corner baths – most of which also had a water jet function which suddenly turned your bath into a low-budget jacuzzi!

IN THE 1990s

In 1990, 68% of UK households owned at least one car, and the use of 'out of town' supermarkets and shopping centres, where just about anything and everything could be purchased in the same area, meant that large weekly or even monthly shops could be done in a single outing and combined with the huge increase in domestic freezers and ready prepared foods, time spent in the kitchen and cooking could be greatly reduced.

Over 80% of households owned a washing machine and 50%, a tumble dryer, so the need to visit the laundrette all but disappeared and instead of "Monday is washing day", the family's laundry could be carried out on an 'as and when' basis. All contributing to an increase in leisure time.

Nearly three-quarters of homes had microwave cookers and for working women who did not want to do their own cleaning, Merry Maids set up their home cleaning franchise in the UK in 1990 and many other companies followed suit.

Commuting

In Great Britain at the beginning of the 1990s, the *average* one-way commute to work was 38 minutes in London, 33 minutes in the south-east, and 21 minutes in the rest of the country. By the end of the decade, full-time workers commuting to and from London, had lost an additional 70 minutes per week of home time to commuting but, by contrast, outside the south-east of Britain, there was no increase in commuting time over the decade. In the south-east, 30% of workers took at least 45 minutes to get to work. In the rest of the country, only 10% did.

Art and Culture

1990 - 1994

1990 In Rome, on the eve of the final of the FIFA World Cup, the Three Tenors sing together for the first time. The event is broadcast live and watched worldwide by millions of people. The highlight is Luciano Pavarotti's performance of Nessun Dorma.
The first Hampton Court Palace Flower Show takes place.

1991 Dame Margot Fonteyn, the Royal Ballet's Prima Ballerina, dies in Panama City, exactly 29 years after her premiere with Rudolf Nureyev who made his debut in 'Giselle'.

1992 Damien Hirst's "Shark", featuring a preserved shark, is first shown at an exhibition at the Saatchi Gallery in London.
Under the new Further and Higher Education Act, Polytechnics are allowed to become new Universities and award degrees of their own.
The last edition of Punch, the UK's oldest satirical magazine since 1841, is published.

1993 Bookmakers cut their odds on the monarchy being abolished by the year 2000 from 100 to 1 to 50 to 1.
QVC launches the first television shopping channel in the UK.

1994 The Duchess of Kent joins the Roman Catholic Church, the first member of the Royal Family to convert to Catholicism for more than 300 years.
The Sunday Trading Act comes into full effect, permitting retailers to trade on Sundays but restricts larger stores to a maximum of six hours, between 10 am and 6 pm.

1995 - 1999

1995 The first ever World Book Day was held on 23rd April, picked to celebrate the anniversary of William Shakespeare's death.

The BBC begins regular Digital Audio Broadcasting from Crystal Palace.

1996 Shortly after publication of the Italian edition of his book 'The Art Forger's Handbook', English-born art forger, Eric Hebborn is beaten to death in Rome.
The Stone of Scone is installed in Edinburgh Castle 700 years after it was removed from Scotland by King Edward I of England.

1997 The Teletubbies caused a sensation when they appeared on BBC TV. They were the most sought-after toy of the year.
The reconstruction of the Elizabethan Globe Theatre, called Shakespeare's Globe opens in London with a production of Shakespeare's 'Henry V'.

1998 Britain's largest sculpture, the Angel of the North by Anthony Gormley is installed at Low Eighton, Gateshead.
More than 15,000 people attend a tribute concert held for Diana, Princess of Wales, at her family home, Althorp Park.

1999 The children's picture book, 'The Gruffalo' by Julia Donaldson is first published.

Media coverage for the Turner Prize was dominated by extreme critical response to Tracey Emin's work 'My Bed' – an installation of her unmade bed, complete with dirty sheets and detritus.

IN THE 1990s

1997: 'Harry Potter and the Philosopher's Stone' by JK Rowling made its debut in June. The initial edition of this first book in the series, comprised 500 copies and the novel has gone on to sell in excess of 120 million. The success of the whole Harry Potter phenomenon is well known, and there have been less expected benefits too. Certainly, before the films, children loved reading the books and boosted the reported numbers of children reading and indeed, reading longer books.

The perception of boarding schools, often associated with misery and cruel, spartan regimes was changed for some by Hogwarts School of Witchcraft and Wizardry. The sense of excitement, community and friendship of the children, the camaraderie of eating together and playing together, made going away to school more appealing for many.

The amazing visual effects used in the films were instrumental in persuading Hollywood to consider UK technical studios and raised the number of visual effects Oscar nominations for British companies significantly.

1997: The Guggenheim Museum of modern and contemporary art, designed by Canadian-American architect Frank Gehry, opened in Bilbao. The building represents an architectural landmark of innovating design, a spectacular structure.

The museum was originally a controversial project. Bilbao's industry, steel and shipbuilding was dying, and the city decided to regenerate to become a modern technological hub of the Basque region, and the controversy was, instead of an office block or factory, the centre piece would be a brand-new art gallery.

It is a spectacular building, more like a sculpture with twisted metal, glass, titanium and limestone, a futuristic setting for fine works of art. The gamble paid off, in the first twenty years, the museum attracted more than 19 million visitors with 70% from outside Spain. Foreign tourists continue to travel through the Basque country bringing a great economic boost to the region and Bilbao itself, has transformed from a grimy post-industrial town to a tourist hotspot.

Films

1990 - 1994

1990 It was Oscar time for an epic western this year and **Dances With Wolves**, directed and starring Kevin Costner with seven Academy Awards, won Best Picture and Best Director. It is one of only three Westerns to win the Oscar for Best Picture, the other two being **Cimmaron** in 1931 and **Unforgotten** in **1992**.

1991 *"Well, Clarice - have the lambs stopped screaming?"* wrote Dr Hannibal Lecter to the young FBI trainee, Clarice Starling. The thriller, **The Silence of the Lambs**, about a cannibalistic serial killer, scared audiences half to death and won the Best Picture Award.

1992 The nominations for the Academy Awards held some serious themes. **The Crying Game** was set against the backdrop of the 'troubles' in Northern Ireland. There was a blind retired Army officer in **Scent of a Woman**, rising troubles in colonial French Vietnam in **Indochine** and the invasion of Panama in **The Panama Deception**.

1993 The acclaimed **Schindler's List** won Best Picture with stiff competition from **The Piano** which won Best Original Screenplay and Robin Williams as **Mrs Doubtfire** which became the second highest grossing film of the year.

1994 Disney's animated musical **The Lion King** made the most money this year, but **Forest Gump** took the prize for Best Picture. The British film **Four Weddings and a Funeral** was a huge success and brought WH Auden's beautiful poem 'Funeral Blues' into the limelight.

1995 - 1999

1995 The tense, amazingly technically correct, story of the ill-fated **Apollo 13** quest to land on the moon failed to win the top Oscar, beaten by Mel Gibson in **Braveheart**, the American take on the story of William Wallace and the first Scottish war of independence against England.

1996 The English Patient a romantic war drama won the Best Picture, up against Mike Leigh's **Secrets and Lies** which won the Best British Film.

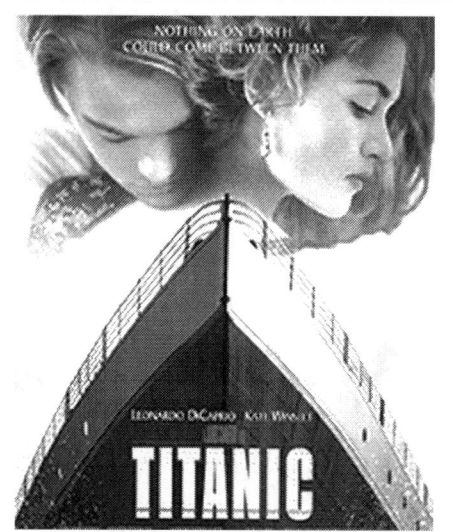

1997 The blockbuster **Titanic** was the film of the year. The combination of romance and disaster proving irresistible. Harland & Wolfe, the builders of RMS Titanic shared blueprints they thought were lost with the crew to produce the scale models, computer-generated imagery and a reconstruction of the ship itself, to re-create the sinking.

1998 Shakespeare in Love, a fictional love affair between Shakespeare and Viola de Lesseps whilst he is writing Romeo and Juliet was hugely popular and won seven Oscars.

1999 In **American Beauty,** Kevin Spacey plays Lester Burnham, an unhappy executive whose midlife awakening is the crux of the story. Bad as he thinks his life is, he cannot not stop seeing the beauty of the world around him.

IN THE 1990s

**"Fear can hold you prisoner,
Hope can set you free."**

In 1994, Tim Robbins and Morgan Freeman starred **The Shawshank Redemption**, an inspirational, life-affirming and uplifting, old-fashioned style prison film and character study in the ilk of 'The Birdman of Alcatraz'. Set in a fictional, oppressive Shawshank State Prison in Maine, two imprisoned men bond over the years, in a tale of friendship, patience, hope, survival and ultimately finding solace and eventual redemption through acts of common decency.

The film was initially a box office disappointment. Many reasons were put forward for its failure at the time, including a general unpopularity of prison films, its lack of female characters and even the title, which was considered to be confusing. However, it was nominated for seven Academy Awards, failed to win a single Oscar, but this raised awareness and increased the film's popularity such that it is now preserved in the US National Film Registry as "culturally, historically, or aesthetically significant".

The Full Monty

In 1997 whilst huge audiences were crying over Kate Winslet and Leonardo di Caprio in **Titanic**, equally huge audiences were laughing at the story of six unemployed men in Sheffield, four of them former steel workers, who are in dire need of cash and who decide to emulate 'The Chippendales' dance, striptease troupe. They devise a dance act with their difference being, that Gaz decides their show must be even better than the originals and declares to the friends that they will go 'the full Monty' – they will strip all the way. Although primarily a comedy, the film touches on several serious subjects too, including unemployment, father's rights – Gaz is unable to pay maintenance to his estranged wife and she is seeking sole custody of his son – and working-class culture, depression and suicide. The film was a huge success as it ultimately is about humanity and the problems people all over the world struggle with.

FASHION

SUPERMODELS

The original supermodels of the 1980s, Linda Evangelista, Naomi Campbell, Christy Turlington and Cindy Crawford were joined later by Claudia Schiffer and then Kate Moss to become the "Big Six". Models used to be categorised as 'print' or 'runway' but the "Big Six" showed that they could do it all, catwalk, print campaigns, magazine covers and even music videos and they became pop 'icons' in their own right. The models were also known for their earning capacity, one famous remark from Linda Evangelista, "We don't wake up for less than $10,000 a day!"

But with the popularity of grunge, came a shift away from the fashion for feminine curves and wholesome looking women, and in came the rise of a new breed of fragile, individual-looking and often younger, models, epitomised by Kate Moss. Her waif-like thinness and delicacy complemented the unkempt look that was popular in the early nineties and a new phrase 'heroin chic' described the down-at-heel settings for fashion shoots presented in magazines. By the end of the decade however, attitudes had shifted and concern about the health of the skeletal model was becoming a source of great debate.

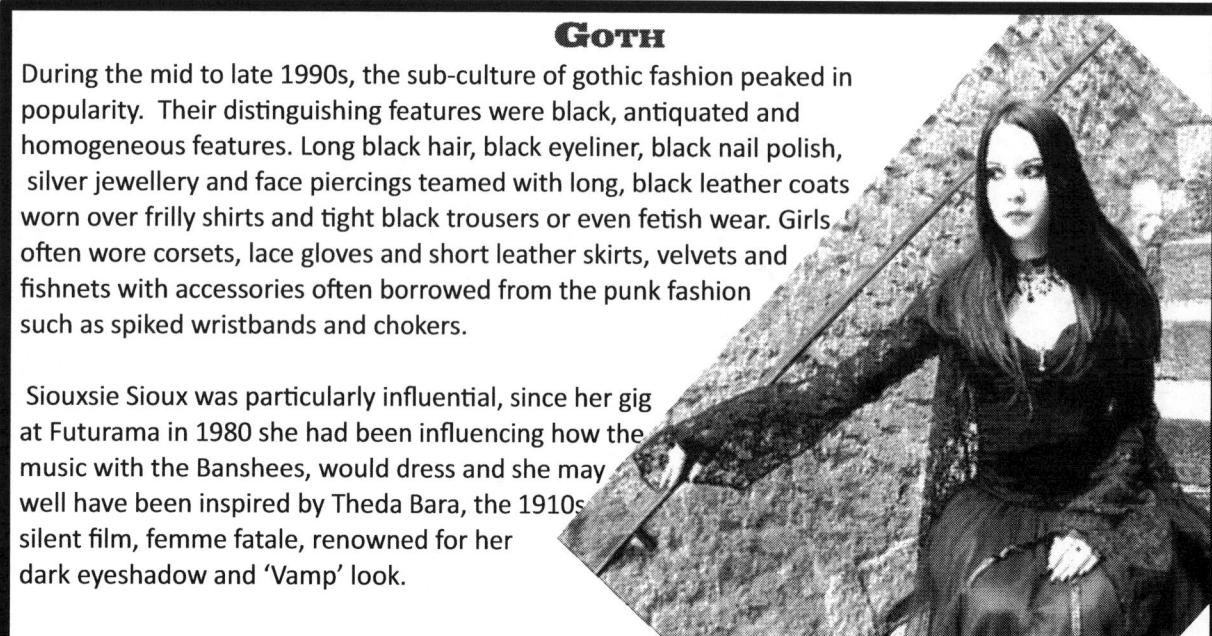

GOTH

During the mid to late 1990s, the sub-culture of gothic fashion peaked in popularity. Their distinguishing features were black, antiquated and homogeneous features. Long black hair, black eyeliner, black nail polish, silver jewellery and face piercings teamed with long, black leather coats worn over frilly shirts and tight black trousers or even fetish wear. Girls often wore corsets, lace gloves and short leather skirts, velvets and fishnets with accessories often borrowed from the punk fashion such as spiked wristbands and chokers.

Siouxsie Sioux was particularly influential, since her gig at Futurama in 1980 she had been influencing how the music with the Banshees, would dress and she may well have been inspired by Theda Bara, the 1910s silent film, femme fatale, renowned for her dark eyeshadow and 'Vamp' look.

IN THE 1990s

GRUNGE

Grunge was a style for the young that emerged in Seattle in the late 1980s and by the early 90s had spread across the world. Made popular by bands such as Nirvana, it was a fashion for both men and women. The look was simple, an oversized flannel shirt, sometimes worn over a t-shirt, and baggy, worn out jeans to give an overall, dishevelled, appearance. The clothes were found ideally in charity shops or at the back of "Dad's wardrobe". A pair of Doc Martens or Converse shoes finished the ensemble.

Nirvana's lead singer Kurt Cobain epitomised the look with holes in his jeans and cardigan sweaters and the fashion world caught on when their second album, 'Nevermind' was released in 1991 and grunge made it onto the catwalk – specifically by Calvin Klein on an 18-year-old Kate Moss. Shrunken baby doll dresses, old prom dresses or even old petticoats and simple slip dresses appeared, often worn with chunky boots and for men, beanies, band t-shirts and knitted sweaters with patterns.

FRIENDS

For women, long loose hair was the most popular women's style, but the most requested hairstyle of the 1990s was said to be 'The Rachel'. Jennifer Anniston's character in 'Friends', Rachel Green, had the haircut people wanted – bouncy, layered, shoulder length, obviously styled to within an inch of its life yet at the same time artfully tousled.

HOODIES

Utilitarian styles such as cargo pants and The Gap's hooded sweatshirts became popular for everyday wear. Industrial and military styles crept into mainstream fashion and camouflage pants were everywhere on the street.
There was also a concerted move towards logoed clothing such as by Tommy Hilfiger

LEISURE

THE GAMES CHILDREN PLAYED

The trend in the 90s was for more electronic, video and computer games but younger children still enjoyed many of the traditional past-times, and events in the 90s such as the FIFA World Cups and the Olympics, produced special collections which reignited interest in collecting 'stickers,' and filling albums.

Crazes were still all the craze too and it was digital pets like Tamagotchi, housed in their small, egg-shaped, handheld video game console that became the biggest fads of the end of the decade.

The Teletubbies caused a huge sensation in 1997, communicating through gibberish and designed to resemble real-life toddlers, they became a huge commercial success, the toy Teletubbies being the most demanded toy of 1997.

However, it was Sony's PlayStation which was the big innovation of the 90s. The first version was able to process games stored on CD-ROMs and introduced 3D graphics to the industry. It had a low retail price and Sony employed aggressive youth marketing. Ridge Racer was the classic motor racing game used in the launch and the popularity of this game was crucial to the early success of the PlayStation.

RESTORATION OF THE SPA

From being at the centre of society in previous times, the spa industry had declined so much that by the 50s, leading spas such as those at Buxton, Cheltenham and Tunbridge Wells had closed. The 1990s saw a simultaneous rise of increasing disposable wealth, and the popularity of a new concept of the spa, pure self-indulgence and pampering.

The need to pause and detox from time to time fitted nicely into the growth of a 'wellness' culture and the understanding of holistic wellbeing, treatments to soothe the mind, body and spirit. Wearing a luxurious white robe and slippers, lounging by a heated pool reading magazines and dipping from time to time into the whirlpools, a trip to the steam room or sauna before taking a light lunch and then unwinding to a fragranced oil body massage because, as L'Oreal had been saying since the 70s, "you're worth it!"

IN THE 1990s

WHERE WE WENT ON HOLIDAY

In the 90s, if we went on a foreign holiday at all, 26m of us in 1996, the norm was to go for just the one, two-week summer break. Booking with a Travel Agent in town or finding a cheap package deal on Teletext, we arrived at our destination with a guide-book, Travellers Cheques and a camera complete with film.

Our favourite places were Spain and France, many of us travelling on the cross-Channel ferries rather than on the budget airlines. Our other favourite hot spots were Belgium, Turkey, Egypt, Kenya and Tunisia.

Although the gap year began in the 1960s, it was in the 1990s when the idea became the 'thing to do' amongst the children of the new wealthy middle classes.

Many visited India, Pakistan and Nepal, Australia, Thailand, the USA and New Zealand being their favoured countries to visit.

Some did voluntary work in the developing nations, building schools and teaching children English.

The 90s saw plenty of new cruise ships being launched for what became a massive growth industry. New cruise lines were formed, and many existing lines merged and Royal Caribbean, Celebrity, Fred Olsen and Carnival, Disney, Silver Sea and Princess lines were all introducing, predominantly older people, to new places and entertaining them royally on the way.

For others, at the opposite end of the cruising scale, was the immensely popular, 'Booze Cruise'. The day trip across the channel to France to stock up on duty free wine and cigarettes.

Music

1990 - 1994

1990 Elton John's **Sacrifice** was initially released as a single in 1989 but only reached No. 55 in the UK. In mid-1990, Radio 1 DJ, Steve Wright began playing it and it soon caught on with other DJs and when re-released as a double A-side single with **Healing Hands** it became John's first solo No 1 single remaining at the top for five weeks.

1991 Cher made the 1960s **Shoop Shoop Song (It's in His Kiss)** an international hit once again. **(Everything I Do) I Do It for You**, from the soundtrack of the film 'Robin Hood: Prince of Thieves' was sung by Bryan Adams and became a huge hit, the best-selling single of the year and stayed at No 1 for 16 weeks.

1992 Shakespeares Sister had their only No 1 UK single hit with **Stay** which stayed at the top for eight consecutive weeks.
The best-selling single of the year was Whitney Houston singing the song written by Dolly Parton, **I Will Always Love You.**

1993 **Pray** by Take That, written by Gary Barlow, was the first of twelve singles by the band to reach No 1 in the UK and the first of a run of four consecutive No 1's.

I'd Do Anything for Love (But I Won't Do That) was the song of the year and won Meat Loaf a Grammy Award for the Best Rock Solo Vocal Performance.

1994 The Most Beautiful Girl in the World by the unpronounceable Love Symbol, or 'The Artist Formerly Known as Prince' reached No 1.
The Manchester United football squad had the help of Status Quo, who wrote and sang along on their two week No 1 hit, **Come on You Reds.**

1995 - 1999

1995 Four artists had two No 1 hits this year. The Outhere Brothers with **Don't Stop (Wiggle Wiggle)** and **Boom Boom Boom**. Take That with **Back for Good** and **Never Forget** and Robson Green & Jerome Flynn with **Unchained Melody/Bluebirds Over the White Cliffs of Dover** – the best seller of the year, and **I Believe/Up On the Roof.**

1996 This was a year with 23 No 1s. Most being at the top for only one week, but Fugees was No 1 twice with the same song **Killing Me Softly.** Firstly, for four weeks in June and then with a break for a week for **Three Lions (Football's Coming Home)** and another week in July.

1997 Elton John topped the charts for five weeks with **Candle in the Wind 1997**, a re-written and re-recorded version of **Candle in the Wind** as a tribute to the late Diana, Princess of Wales.
Another kind of tribute, this time to the popularity of the Teletubbies, their **Teletubbies say 'Eh-oh!'** stayed at No 1 for two weeks in December.

1998 The main soundtrack song from the blockbuster film Titanic provided Celine Dion with a hit, **My Heart Will Go On.**
Cher reinvented herself, and her song, **Believe** stayed at No 1 for seven weeks and was the year's best seller.

1999 Britney Spears made her debut single with **...Baby One More Time** which became a worldwide hit and sold over ten million copies.
Cliff Richard's **Millenium Prayer** is knocked off its 3 weeks at No 1 spot just in time for the boy band, Westlife, to make the Christmas No 1 with **I Have a Dream/Seasons in the Sun.**

IN THE 1990s

COOL BRITANNIA

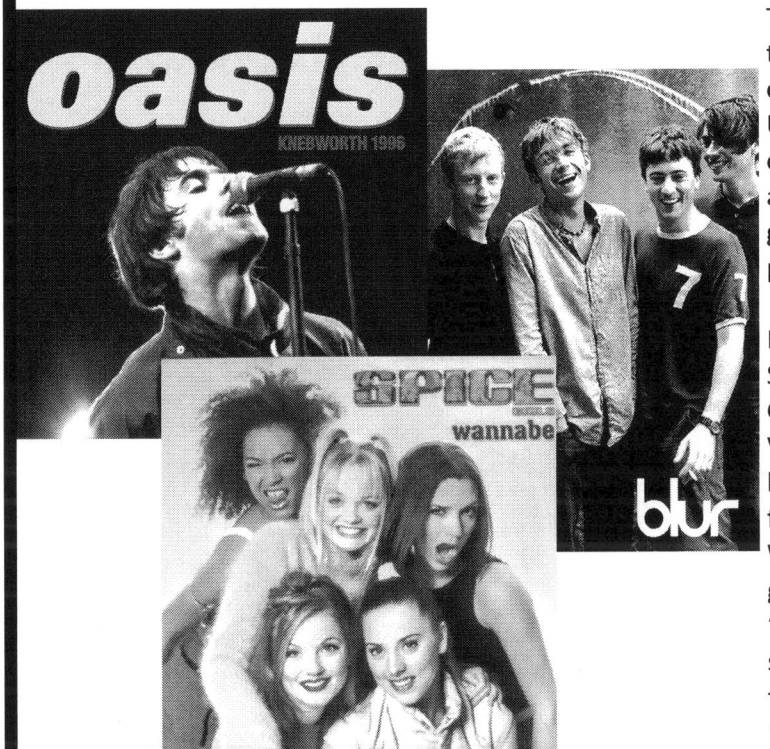

Throughout the mid and second half of the 1990s, Cool Britannia was a period of increased pride in the culture of the UK inspired by the 'Swinging London' of the 1960s pop culture. This brought about a huge success of 'Britpop' with groups such as Blur and Oasis and particularly, the Spice Girls.

Mel B, 'Scary Spice', Melanie C, 'Sporty Spice', Emma Bunton, 'Baby Spice', Geri Halliwell, 'Ginger Spice' and Victoria Beckham, 'Posh Spice' brought girl power to the fore. Their first single was 1996's iconic **Wannabe**, which established the group as a global phenomenon as 'Spice Mania' circled the globe. They scored the Christmas Number 1 single three years in a row and had nine UK No 1's in total.

LOVE IS ALL AROUND

In June 1994, Wet Wet Wet the Scottish soft rock band had a huge international hit, with 15 weeks as the UK No 1, with their cover of the 1960s hit by The Troggs, **Love Is All Around.** Their version was used on the soundtrack of the blockbuster film 'Four Weddings and a Funeral'.

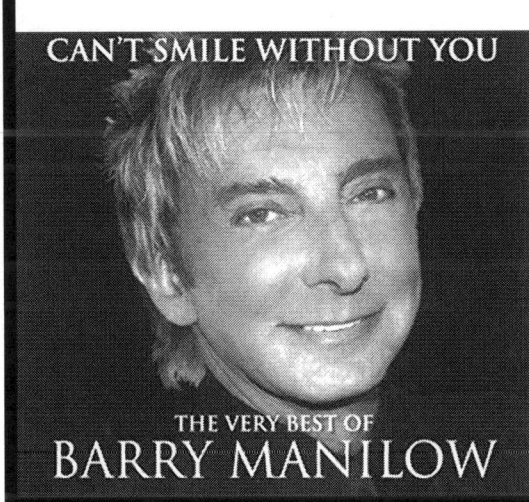

Richard Curtis, the director of the film, had approached Wet Wet Wet with a choice of three cover songs to record for the soundtrack, the other two being **I Will Survive** by Gloria Gaynor and Barry Manilow's **Can't Smile Without You**.

103

SCIENCE AND NATURE

The Hubble Telescope

The Hubble telescope is a general-purpose orbiting observatory. Orbiting approximately 380 mi (612 km) above Earth, the 12.5-ton Hubble Space Telescope has peered farther into the universe than any telescope before it. The Hubble, which was launched on April 24, 1990, has produced images with unprecedented resolution at visible, near-ultraviolet, and near-infrared wavelengths since its originally faulty optics were corrected in 1993.

Although ground-based telescopes are finally starting to catch up, the Hubble continues to produce a stream of unique observations. During the 1990s and now into the 2000s, the Hubble has revolutionised the science of astronomy, becoming one, if not the most, important instruments ever used in astronomy.

Add To Basket

The first ever shopper bought online from Tesco in 1984 using her television remote control, but it was in 1990s, following the creation by Tim Berners-Lee of the World Wide Web server and browser and the commercialisation of the internet in 1991 giving birth to e-commerce, that online shopping really began to take off.

In 1995, Amazon began selling books online, computer companies started using the internet for *all* their transactions and Auction Web was set up by Pierre Omidyar as a site *"dedicated to bringing together buyers and sellers in an honest and open marketplace."* We now know this as eBay and we can buy just about anything on Amazon.

Comparison sites were set up in 1997 and in 1998, PayPal was founded, the way to pay online without having to share your financial information. By 1999, online only shops were beginning to emerge and paved the way for 'Click for Checkout' to become commonplace.

IN THE 1990s

THE KYOTO PROTOCOL

In December 1997, at the instigation of the United Nations, representatives from 160 countries met in Kyoto, Japan, to discuss climate change and draft the Kyoto Protocol which aimed to restrict the greenhouse gas emissions associated with global warming.

The protocol focused on demands that 37 developed nations work to reduce their greenhouse gas emissions placing the burden on developed nations, viewing them as the primary sources and largely responsible for carbon emissions.

Developing nations were asked only to comply voluntarily, exempted from the protocol's requirements. The protocol's approach included establishing a 'carbon credits system' whereby nations can earn credits by participating in emission reduction projects in other nations. A carbon credit is a tradeable permit or certificate that provides the holder

SHOCK WAVES

A large earthquake, by British standards, occurred near Bishop's Castle, Shropshire on the Welsh Borders on 2 April 1990 at 13:46 GMT. With a magnitude of 5.1, the shock waves were felt over a wide area of Britain, from Ayrshire in the north to Cornwall in the south, Kent in the east and Dublin in the west.

Worldwide in 1990, there were 18 quakes of magnitude 7.0 or above and 134 quakes between 6.0 and 7.0, 4435 quakes between 4.0 and 5.0, 2755 quakes between 3.0 and 4.0, and 8618 quakes between 2.0 and 3.0. There were also 29800 quakes below magnitude 2.0 which people don't normally feel.

The strongest quake was north of Pulau Hulawa Island in Indonesia, registering 7.8 on the Richter scale.

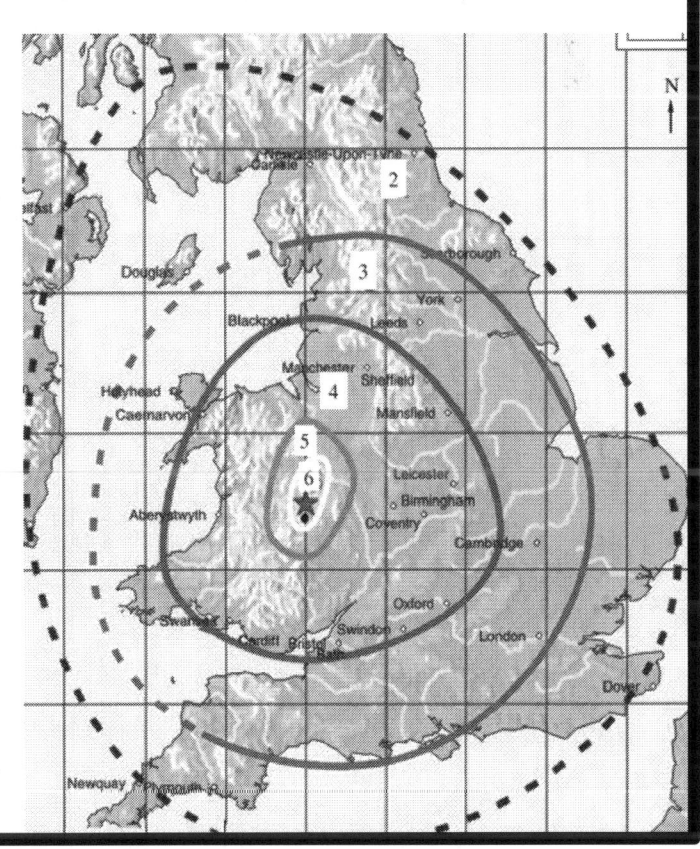

105

SPORT

1990 - 1994

1990 West Germany won the **FIFA World Cup** in Rome, defeating defending champions Argentina, 1–0 in the final.
The British golfer, Nick Faldo, had an amazing year, winning both the **Masters** and the Claret Jug at the **Open** at St Andrews, and capturing the PGA Player of the Year award, the first non-American to do so.

1991 At the **World Athletics** Championships in Tokyo, Mike Powell broke the 23 year-long world record **long jump** set by Bob Beamon, with a jump of 29' 4½".

1992 The rugby, **Five Nations Championship** is won by England who complete the Grand Slam for the second consecutive year.

The summer **Olympics** are held in Barcelona, Spain where Sally Gunnell takes home gold in the Women's 400 metres hurdles, Linford Christie triumphs in the Men's 100 metres, and rowers Matthew Pinsent and Steve Redgrave finish first in the Men's coxless pair, the first Olympic gold for all four athletes. In the **Paralympics**, Tanni Grey-Thompson in her debut Games, takes home four golds and a silver.

1993 Manchester United win the inaugural **English Premier League** title, their first league title in 26 years.
Shane Warne bowls the so-called 'Ball of the Century' in the first Test at Old Trafford. With his first ball against England, in his first **Ashes**, he bowled Mike Gatting out.

1994 Tiger Woods becomes the youngest man ever to win the **U.S. Amateur Golf Championships**, at age 18.
George Foreman becomes **Boxing's** oldest Heavyweight Champion at forty-five.

1995 - 1999

1995 In motor racing, Michael Schumacher wins his second consecutive **Drivers' Championship**, and Benetton wins its first and only Constructors' Championship.
British triple jumper Jonathan Edwards sets a world record in the **Athletics World Championships**, jumping 60' (18.29 m).

1996 The 95/96 **Rugby League** ends with Wigan declared champions.
Stephen Hendry wins the **World Snooker Championship** and remains the world number one.

1997 At 21, Tiger Woods becomes the youngest **Masters** winner in history, as well as the first non-white winner at Augusta. He set the scoring record at 270 and the record for the largest margin of victory at 12 strokes.

1998 In Japan, **Curling** is included in the Winter Olympics for the first time.

1999 Pete Sampras beats his biggest rival, Andre Agassi in the **Wimbledon Men's Singles** Final giving him his sixth win at the All England Club.
In the **US Open Tennis** final, at the age of 17, Serena Williams beats the number one player Martina Hingis and marks the beginning of one of the most dominant careers in the history of women's tennis.

IN THE 1990s

THE DANGEROUS SIDE TO SPORT

By 1993, Monica Seles, the Serbian-American tennis player, had won eight Grand Slam titles and was ranked No. 1 in the world. On April 30, 1993, then just 19, she was sitting on a courtside seat during a changeover in a match in Hamburg when a German man, said later to be a fan of the tennis star's German rival, Steffi Graf, leaned over a fence and stabbed her between the shoulder blades with a knife. The assailant was quickly apprehended and Seles was taken to the hospital with a wound half and inch deep in her upper back. She recovered from her physical injuries but was left with deep emotional scars and didn't play again professionally for another two years.

Leading up to the 1994 Winter Olympics, figure skater Nancy Kerrigan was attacked during a practice session. This had been 'commissioned' by the ex-husband of fellow skater, Tonya Harding and her bodyguard. Kerrigan was Harding's long-time rival and the one person in the way of her making the Olympic team, and she was desperate to win. Fortunately for Kerrigan, the injury left her with just bruises – no broken bones but she had to withdraw from the U.S. Figure Skating Championship the following night. However, she was still given a spot on the Olympic team and finished with a silver medal. Harding finished in eighth place and later had her U.S. Figure Skating Championship title revoked and was banned from the United States Figure Skating Association for life.

Also in 1994, Andrés Escobar the Colombian footballer, nicknamed ' The Gentleman' - known for his clean style of play and calmness on the pitch - was murdered following a second-round match against the US in the FIFA World Cup. This was reportedly in retaliation for Escobar having scored an own goal which contributed to the team's elimination from the tournament.

In 1997, Evander Holyfield and Mike Tyson's fight made headlines after Tyson was disqualified for biting off a part of his rival's ear, an infamous incident that would lead to the event being dubbed "The Bite Fight".

TRANSPORT

HAULAGE

The 1990s was a decade devoted to environmental considerations for haulage with top priority given to cleaner emissions and low noise levels. By the end of the decade, integrated IT solutions were being used to provide the tools necessary to increase efficiency and safety.

A significant factor in the 1990s was making the lorry more aerodynamic. A 20% saving in fuel consumption meant lower emissions and also the average transport operator could improve profits by up to 50%.

CRUISE SHIPS

The largest passenger ship of the 1990s was Royal Caribbean's 'Voyager of the Seas' at 137,276 gross tonnage and 310 m (1,020 ft) long.

This record was held between Oct 1999 and Sep 2000, when it was superseded by 'Explorer of the Seas', larger by only 12 GT. Royal Caribbean have, on order, and due 2024, an Oasis class cruiser of 231,000 gross tonnage, 362 m(1,188 ft) long.

THE HIGHWAY CODE

In July 1996 a separate written theory test was introduced to the Driving Test in the UK to replace questions asked about 'The Highway Code' whilst actually driving. Learner drivers were expected to know rather different information then from that published in the first edition of the Highway Code, price 1d, launched in 1931.

• In 1931 mirrors were not even mentioned.

• Drivers were advised to sound their horn when overtaking.

• At least 8 pages showed the various hand signals a driver should use. There was a single page in the current edition.

• Contained 18 pages (out of 24) of advice, compared to 135 pages in 2007.

• Included advice to drivers of horse drawn vehicles to 'rotate the whip above the head; then incline the whip to the right or left to show the direction in which the turn is to be made'.

It wasn't until the second edition of the Code that diagrams of road signs appeared, just 10 in all, plus a warning about the dangers of driving when tired or drinking and driving.

108

IN THE 1990s

Renault Clio

Advertising for the first-generation Renault Clio introduced us to 'Nicole *et* Papa' and gave the small car a personality that appealed to drivers of all ages.

Ford Focus

The Focus replaced the previously very successful Escort. Ford wanted a 'World Car' to sell across all markets so the Focus was born and is still produced.

Toyota Previa

Toyota created the multi- purpose vehicle market with the Spacecruiser in the 80s, but the futuristic replacement, the Toyota Previa was a whole new approach to the people carrier.

Lexus LS 400

Toyota moved into the luxury market with the Lexus brand. The Lexus' flagship model is one of the most reliable vehicles ever built.

COCOTAXI

The auto-rickshaw began in Havana in the 1990s and soon spread to the whole of Cuba. These gas-scooters are named after their shape, that of a coconut and are made of a fibreglass shell with seats welded onto it. They can travel at about 30mph and because they are small, they weave and squeeze in and out of the city traffic. Blue Cocotaxis are for locals, yellow for tourists.

MOTORCYCLES

During the 1990s motorcycles started to evolve more quickly and there was a resurgence in the British biking industry with Triumph starting up production.

A bike lovers favourite however, was the 1995, Aprilia RS250.

New Year's Eve 1999
The Millennium Bug

Whilst the world was getting 'ready to party' there was an undercurrent of anxiety about the Y2K (year 2000) Bug and many people were scared. When complicated computer programmes were first written in the 1960s, programmers used a two-digit code for the year, leaving out the "19." As the year 2000 approached, many believed that the systems would not interpret the "00" correctly, making the year 2000 indistinguishable from 1900 causing a major malfunction.

It was particularly worrying to certain organisations. Banks calculate the rate for interest owed daily and instead of the rate for one day, if the 'clocks went back' their computers would calculate a rate of interest for **minus** 100 years!

Airlines felt they were at a very great risk. All scheduled flights are recorded on computers and liable to be affected and, if the computer reverted to 1900, well, there were very few airline flights that year!
Power plants were threatened, depending on routine computer maintenance for safety checks, such as water pressure or radiation levels, the wrong date would wreck the calculations and possibly put nearby residents at risk.

Huge sums were spent to prepare for the consequences and both software and hardware companies raced to fix it by developing "Y2K compliant" programmes. Midnight passed on the 1 January 2000 and the crisis failed to materialise - planes did not fall from the sky, power stations did not melt down and thousands of people who had stocked up on food, water, even arms, or purchased backup generators or withdrawn large sums of money in anticipation of a computer-induced apocalypse, could breathe easily again.

The Millennium Dome

Officially called the O2, the huge construction and tourist attraction alongside the Thames in Greenwich, London was initially built to house an exhibition for the approach of the 21st Century. Designed by Sir Richard Rogers, the central dome is the largest in the world. On December 31, 1999, a New Year's Eve celebration at the dome was attended by some 10,500 people, including the Prime Minister, Tony Blair, and the Queen. Opening the next day, the Millennium Dome exhibition lasted until December 31, 2000.

And A New Millennium
Memorabilia and Monuments

The Millennium Wheel Better known as the London Eye, at 135m (443 ft) it is Europe's tallest cantilevered observation wheel. Situated on the South Bank of the Thames when opened it used to offer the highest public viewing point in London until superseded in 2013 by the 245m high (804 ft) observation deck on the 72nd floor of The Shard.

Portsmouth's Millennium Tower opened five years late and officials were so concerned that people may actually have forgotten what the millennium was, that they gave it a new name, **The Spinnaker Tower**.

The Millennium Bridge is a steel suspension bridge for pedestrians over the River Thames linking Bankside with the City of London. Londoners nicknamed it the "Wobbly Bridge" after pedestrians experienced an alarming swaying motion on its opening day.

Lots of memorabilia was produced to mark the new millennium. Some pieces are timeless classics and others will soon be forgotten.

KEY EVENTS 2000-2009

2000:
Jan: Celebrations take place throughout the UK on the 1st and the Millennium Dome is officially opened by The Queen.

Aug 4th: Queen Elizabeth the Queen Mother celebrates her hundredth birthday

2001:
Feb: The Foot and Mouth disease crisis begins. Over 6 million cows and sheep are killed to halt the disease.

Jun: Labour wins the General Election. David Cameron is a new entrant, Edward Heath retires, and William Hague resigns as leader of the Conservatives.

2002:
Jan: The Euro is officially introduced in the Eurozone countries.

Jun: The Golden Jubilee. A special service is held in St Paul's Cathedral to mark the Queen's 50 years on the throne. Celebrations take place all over the country.

2003:
Mar: The United States, along with coalition forces primarily from the United Kingdom, initiates war on Iraq

May: BBC Radio 4 airs a report stating that the government claimed in its dossier, that Iraq could deploy weapons of mass destruction within forty-five minutes knowing the claim to be dubious.
Jul: Dr David Kelly, the weapons expert who was the reporter's source, is found dead.

2004:
Jan: The Hutton Inquiry into the circumstances of the death of Dr Kelly is published. The UK media, in general, condemns the report as a whitewash.

Jul: A new Countryside Code is published in advance of the 'Right to Roam' coming into effect in September across England and Wales.

TERRORISM

2001: On the 11th September, Al-Qaeda terrorists hijack civilian airliners and fly two into the Twin Towers of the World Trade Centre in New York, which collapse. There are 3,000 fatalities including 67 British nationals.

SOCIAL MEDIA

2004: In February, Mark Zuckerberg launches 'The Facebook', later renamed 'Facebook' as an online social networking website for Harvard University Students. In 2006 it was opened up to anyone over the age of 13.

21st Century

Explosion

2005: On the morning of 11 December, the UK experienced its largest explosion since World War Two. A huge blast at the Buncefield fuel depot in Hemel Hempstead, was heard as far away as the Netherlands and caused the UK's biggest blaze in peacetime which shrouded much of south-east England in smoke.

High Speed Trains

2007: In November, the Queen officially opened 'High Speed 1' and 'St Pancras International' station. The Channel Tunnel first opened to Eurostar in 1994, with trains running from Waterloo, but the new 69-mile link meant the journey from London to Paris reduced to 2 hrs 15 minutes and to Brussels 1 hr 51 min.

2005:
Apr: Prince Charles marries Camilla Parker Bowles at a private ceremony at Windsor Guildhall.

Aug: Hurricane Katrina devastates much of the U.S. Gulf Coast from Louisiana to the Florida Panhandle killing an estimated 1,836 people

2006:
Jul: Twitter is launched, becoming one of the largest social media platforms in the world.

Nov: Alexander Litvinenko a British-naturalised Russian defector dies of polonium poisoning in London.

2007:
Jun: Tony Blair resigns as Prime Minister and Gordon Brown is elected unopposed.

Jul: England introduces a ban on smoking in enclosed public places in line with Scotland, Wales and N. Ireland.

2008:
Mar: Terminal 5 is opened at London Heathrow but IT problems cause over 500 flights to be cancelled

Nov: St Hilda's College admits male undergraduates and ceases to be the last single-sex college at Oxford.

Dec: Woolworths shuts down in the UK.

2009:
Jul: The largest haul of Anglo-Saxon treasure ever found, the Staffordshire Hoard, is first uncovered buried beneath a field near Litchfield. 4,600 items amounting to 11 lb of gold, 3lb of silver and 3.5k pieces of garnet cloisonné jewellery.

Oct: The independent audit of MPs expenses is completed and exposes a widespread parliamentary scandal.

KEY EVENTS 2010-2019

2010:
Jan: In the Chilcott Inquiry, set up in 2009, Tony Blair is questioned in public for the first time about his decision to take the UK to war against Iraq.

May: The General Election results in a Hung Parliament. An alliance is formed between the Tories and the Liberal Democrats.

2011:
Feb: An earthquake of 6.3 magnitude devastates Christchurch, New Zealand. Hundreds of people are killed.

Apr: Prince William marries Catherine Middleton in Westminster Abbey.

2012:
Jun: The UK begins celebrations of the Queen's Diamond Jubilee. Events include a pageant on the Thames and a Pop Concert outside Buckingham Palace

Jul: The summer Olympic Games are held in London, making it the first city to host them for a third time.

2013:
Jul: A new Marriage Act receives Royal Assent and same-sex marriage becomes legal in England and Wales.

Aug: A burger, grown from bovine stem cells in a laboratory, is cooked and eaten in London. The same month, a 15 ton 'fatburg' is removed after completely blocking a London sewer.

2014:
Mar: Prince Harry launches the Invictus Games for wounded soldiers.

Mar: The first gay weddings take place in England and Wales.

THE SHARD

2012: In July, The Shard, an iconic 'vertical city' is officially opened in London. It is the tallest building in Europe and the tallest habitable free-standing structure in the UK at 1,016ft (309.6 m)

THE ARAB SPRING

2010: 'The Arab Spring', a series of anti-government protests, uprisings, and armed rebellions spread across much of the Arab world. Starting in Tunisia it spread to Libya, Egypt, Yemen, Syria and Bahrain. Amongst leaders to be deposed was Gaddafi of Libya.

21st Century

BREXIT

June 2016: After months of heated, angry argument and debate, the referendum on whether to leave the EU or remain within it, is held. Nearly 30m people take part and the result is to leave the EU: 51.9% votes to 48.1%.

March 2017: Article 50 is invoked and the two-year countdown to departure begins.
March 2019: Parliament rejected Theresa May's EU withdrawal agreement and a new deadline is set by The European Council to leave, with or without an Agreement, at the end of Oct 2019.
Jun 2019: Unable to 'deliver Brexit', Theresa May steps down and in Jul 2019: Boris Johnson becomes Prime Minister.
Oct 2019: The deadline to leave passes, and the EU agrees to a new date, end of Jan 2020. Commemorative Brexit coins are melted down.
Jan 2020: Johnson signs the Withdrawal Agreement.

January 31st 2020: At 11pm, the UK leaves the European Union and marks the moment with a party in Parliament Square.

2015:
Jan: Two Al-Qaeda gunmen kill 12 and injure 11 more at the Paris headquarters of the satirical newspaper Charlie Hebdo.

May: The General Election is won by David Cameron for the Conservatives with an outright majority of 331 seats.
Jun: The 800th anniversary of the Magna Carta.

2016:
Jun: The UK Referendum to leave the EU, Brexit, takes place and the majority vote is 'Yes'. David Cameron later resigns.
Jul: On July 14, Bastille Day (Independence Day), a terrorist drives a truck through a crowded promenade in Nice, France. 87 people are killed.
Nov: Donald Trump becomes US President.

2017:
There are a string of deadly terror attacks in Britain including : Westminster Bridge, the Manchester Arena and London Bridge.
Jun: The Tories lose their majority in Theresa May's general election gamble.

2018:
Apr: The UK, France, and United States order the bombing of Syrian military bases.

May: Prince Harry marries the American actress Meghan Markle in St George's Chapel, Windsor Castle. It is thought 1.9m people watched on TV worldwide.

2019:
Jun: Theresa May resigns as Prime Minister. Before she goes, she agrees a new legally binding target to reach net zero by 2050.
Jul: Boris Johnson becomes Prime Minister.

115

FILMS & THE ARTS

"One Ring to Rule Them All'

Based on the fantasy, adventure epics written by JRR Tolkein in the 1930s and 40s, Peter Jackson's trilogy of films became a major financial success, received widespread acclaim and is ranked among the greatest film trilogies ever made. The three films were shot simultaneously in Jackson's native New Zealand between 1999 and 2000 and with a budget of $281m, was one of the most ambitious film projects ever undertaken.

The **Lord of the Rings: The Fellowship of the Ring** was nominated for 13 Oscars and won four, one of which, unsurprisingly, was for the Special Effects as did **The Lord of the Rings: The Two Towers** and **The Lord of the Rings: The Return of the King**.

Peter Jackson then went on to make a further three films based on Tolkein's Middle Earth saga, **'The Hobbit: An Unexpected Journey, The Hobbit: The Desolation of Smaug** and **The Hobbit: The Battle of the Five Armies**. The three films were prequels to the Lord of the Rings saga and together, the six films became one of the 'greatest movie series franchise' of all time.

'The Greatest Fairy Tale Never Told'

In 2002, the Oscar for Best Animated Feature was awarded for the first time to **Shrek**, the large, surly, sarcastic, wisecracking, Scottish-accented greenish ogre with a round face and stinky breath who took a mud shower outdoors near his home in the swamp and blew fart bubbles in a mud pool! But being a goodhearted ogre, children and adults alike, loved him!

'A Film of Our Times'

The Social Network made in 2010, is an American biographical drama portraying the founding of the social networking phenomenon Facebook and the resulting lawsuits. Based on the book, 'The Accidental Billionnaires' by Ben Mezrich the film was nominated for the Oscars in 2011 winning The Best Adapted Screenplay but missing out on Best Picture to **The King's Speech.**

In The 21st Century

'Precious Pieces'

In 2007 Damien Hirst wowed the art-world with his fabulous **For the Love of God** a life-size platinum cast of an eighteenth century human skull, covered by 8,601 flawless diamonds, inset with the original skull's teeth. At the front of the cranium is a 52.4 carat pink diamond. The work is reputed to be the most expensive contemporary artwork ever made and was *allegedly* entitled **For the Love of God** in response to a question posed by the artist's mother "For the love of God, what are you going to do next?"! It has become one of the most widely recognised works of contemporary art and represents the artist's continued interest in mortality and the fragility of life.

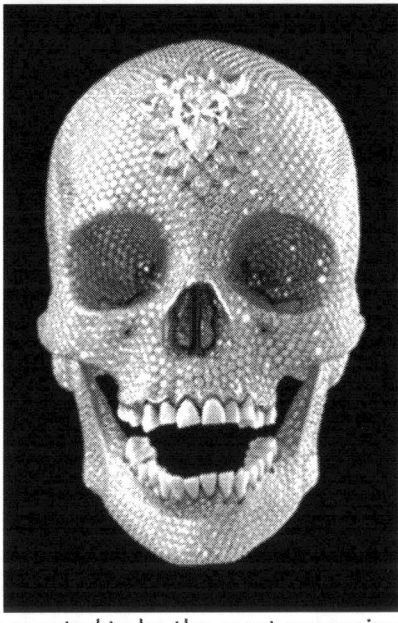

Screaming Success

In May, 2012, a pastel version of **The Scream**, by Norwegian painter Edvard Munch, sells for $120m in New York City, setting a new world record for a work of art at auction.

'Question Everything, Believe Nothing'

Conspiracy theory is not a new phenomenon but in 2001, Dan Brown introduced the world to Robert Langdon and a whole new collection of conspiracies and secret societies, with his first book, **Angels & Demons**. Set in the Vatican and Rome, Langdon must decipher a labyrinthine trail of ancient symbols if he is to defeat the Illuminati, a monstrous secret brotherhood.

When **The Da Vinci Code** came along in 2003, hordes of tourists descended on Paris, staring at the Mona Lisa as though she held the secret to life and traipsing around cathedrals and monuments, speculating on the Holy Grail and obsessed with the Priory of Sion and Opus Dei.

By 2009 in **The Lost Symbol**, Brown had set his sights on the Capitol Building, Washington DC and the shadowy, mythical world in which the Masonic secrets abound.

Back in Italy in 2013, this time Florence, for **Inferno**, Langdon is also back to hidden passageways and ancient secrets that lie behind historic facades, deciphering a sequence of codes buried deep within Renaissance artworks with only the help of a few lines from Dante's Inferno.

Music In The

The Top Ten UK Singles of the 21st Century

YEAR
- 2013 **Happy** by Pharrell Williams.
- 2002 Will Young's **Anything is Possible**
- 2013 **Blurred Lines** sung by Robin Thicke featuring TI and Pharrell Williams.
- 2014 Mark Ronson and featuring Bruno Mars with **Uptown Funk**
- 2011 Adele singing **Someone Like You**
- 2011 **Moves Like Jagger** by Maroon 5 featuring Christina Aguilera
- 2012 Gotye featuring Kimbra and **Somebody That I Used to Know**
- 2013 **Wake Me Up** by Avicii
- 2009 The Black Eyed Peas with **I Gotta Feeling**
- 2013 Daft Punk featuring Pharrell Williams and **Get Lucky**

First of the Century

The first No 1 Single of the 21st Century in the UK Charts is **Manic Street Preachers** with The Masses Against the Classes. This song by Welsh rock band was released as a limited-edition single being deleted, removed from wholesale supply, on the day of release. Despite this, it peaked at No 1.

Since 2014 streaming has counted towards sales, called "combined sales", at the rate of 100 streams equal to one download or physical purchase, although the singles chart no longer uses this ratio. The biggest selling song of the 21st Century, based on combined physical, download and streaming sales, *and as of Sep 2017*, is **The Shape of You** by Ed Sheeran, (2017) with sales of just over 3 million.

Millennial Music

What about the music the Millennials, born in the 80s and 90s, like to listen to? It may eventually fit just as well onto a "best songs of all time" playlist alongside the likes of The Beatles and The Supremes. These are some of the 21st-century pop songs that could stand the test of time and they are all female artists too!
Single Ladies (Put a Ring on It) by Beyoncé. **Umbrella** by Rihanna featuring Jay-Z. **Shake it Off** by Taylor Swift. **Toxic** by Britney Spears. **Rolling in the Deep** by Adele and **Firework** by Katy Perry.

However, those of from the 'Good Old Days' are not surprised to know, that in 2019, a US study found that golden oldies stick in millennials' minds far more than the relatively bland, homogeneous pop of today. A golden age of popular music lasted from the 1960s to the 1990s, academics claimed. Songs from this era proved to be much more memorable than tunes released in the 21st century.

21st Century

Fashion

Music and fashion have been intertwined since the 1960s and nothing appears to be changing at the beginning of the 21st Century. The young will imitate their idols. Today though, designers are taking their inspiration from the past and bringing it back into the future, the new millennium fashion is a 'fusion' of the 60's, 70's and 80's, feeding our freedom to 'wear what we want, whenever we want'.

However, one major shift of emphasis will be the consumer's demand for environmental sustainability and social responsibility and to move away from 'fast, disposable fashion'. Fashion began moving at breakneck speeds in the 1960´s, and the young wanted cheaply made clothing to follow these new trends. Fashion brands had to find ways to keep up with the ever-increasing demand for affordable clothing and this led to the massive growth in manufacturing being outsourced to the developing world, saving us millions of pounds in labour costs.

In the 21st Century we are aware of dreadful labour practices and the enormous amounts of waste. The industry will need to slow down for the customer mindful of how their clothes are made.

Science & Technology

Watch everywhere.
Stream unlimited movies and TV shows on your phone, tablet, laptop, and TV without paying more.

The technological innovations of the first two decades of the 21st century have drastically revolutionised people's day-to-day lives. Television, radio, paperback novels, cinemas, landline telephones and even letter writing can be, and have been by millions, replaced by connected devices, digital books, Netflix, and communications using apps such as Twitter, Facebook or Snapchat. We have marvels such as personalized hover boards, self-driving cars and, of course, the smartphone. All commonplace now when just a decade and a half ago most were unfathomable.

Consumers watch films, listen to music, record the day, book holidays and carry out their shopping with a few taps on a screen and even people who have never owned a computer are digitally connected 24-hours a day via their smartphones.

E-readers and Kindle

E-readers have been under development since the 1940s, but it was not until 2004 when Sony first brought out an e-reader, and then, when demand for e-books increased, Kindle arrived in 2007, that they became mainstream. An eBook is a text-based publication in digital form stored as electronic files. E-readers are small, convenient, light and have a huge storage capacity that allows for reading whilst travelling, making electronic notes and character summaries and more. Pages do not exist in eBooks and where the reader is 'up to' is altered depending on what font size and layout the reader has chosen, which means 'your place' is displayed as a percentage of the whole text.

Although it was feared e-readers were the death knell for the traditional book, it appears not to be the case as it seems many people really do like to hold a physical book in their hands, feeling the weight. After all, even Kindle uses a **'bookmark'** to hold our place!

3D Printing

The 3D printer has been around since the 1980s. Now, the know-how is getting used for everything from automobile components to bridges to much less painful ballet slippers, synthetic organs, custom dental work, prosthetic limbs, and custom hearing aids.

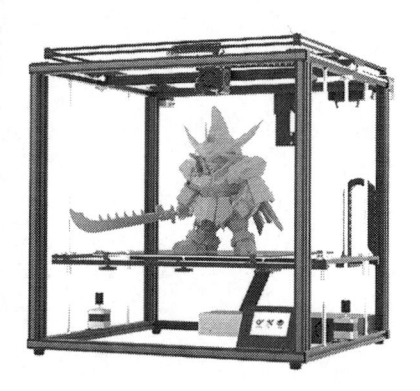

In The 21st Century

The Future of Transport

Driverless Cars
Self-driving cars are expected to be on the roads more quickly, and in greater numbers, than was anticipated.

Floating Trains
There are already Maglev – magnetic levitation – trains in use. The Shanghai Maglev connects their Airport with a station on the outskirts of the city. At speeds up to 268 mph.

Hyperloop
High speed bullet trains or transport capsules are being developed to provide unprecedented speeds of 600mph.

Solar Panel Roads
Which also generate electricity are being tested in, amongst other countries, France, the US and China as well as on bike lanes in the Netherlands.

Touch Screens

Smartphones, tablets, and even Smartwatches all need one underlying technology without which they cannot succeed. The touch screen, as we know it integrated into consumer products, took off in the 2000s and is now everywhere, homes, cars, restaurants, shops, planes, wherever. Unlike other computer devices, touchscreens are unique because they allow the user to interact directly with what's on the screen, unlike a mouse that moves a cursor.

In 2007, the original iPhone was released and revolutionised the phone industry, its touchscreen can change between a dialling pad, a keyboard, a video, a game, or a myriad of other apps. The Apple iPad was released in 2010 and with it, a wave of tablets from competitors. Not only are most of our phones equipped with touchscreens, but portable computers are too.

Sport In The

2000 Tiger Woods wins the **US Open** golf by 15 shots, a record for all majors.
Australia wins the **Rugby League World Cup** against New Zealand. Italy joins the Five Nations **Rugby Union** making it the Six Nations.

2001 Sir Donald Bradman dies. He retains the highest **Test Match** batting average of 99.94.
Venus Williams wins the **Ladies Singles Final at Wimbledon**.

2002 "Lewis–Tyson: Is On". Lennox won the fight by a knockout to retain the **WBC Heavyweight Boxing** Crown.
Arsenal matched Manchester United with their third Double, **FA Cup** and **League title**.

2003 Mike Wier becomes the first Canadian and the first *left-handed golfer* to win the **Masters**.
Serena Williams beats her sister Venus in the **Ladies Singles Final at Wimbledon**.

2004 In Athens, Kelly Holmes wins **Olympic Gold** for the 800 & 1500m. Britain also win Gold in the 4x100m relay. Michael Schumacher, in his Ferrari, wins a record 12 of the first 13 races of the season, and wins the **F1** World Drivers Championship.

2005 Ellen MacArthur attains the World Record for **Sailing** the fastest solo circumnavigation of the globe.
In **Cricket**, England win The Ashes.

2006 Justin Gatlin equals Powell's **100m world record** time of 9.77 seconds in Quatar.
In golf, Europe wins the **Ryder Cup** for the third straight time, defeating the USA 18½–9½.

2007 27 January – After nearly 50 years, the final edition of **'Grandstand'**, the BBC flagship sports programme is aired.
Australia completes a 5–0 whitewash over England in the **Ashes Series**, the first time since 1920–21 that one team has won all the Tests in the series.

2008 At the Beijing Olympics, Team GB dominate the **Cycling**, winning 14 medals, including 8 Gold.
Usain Bolt thundered to victory in the **100m Olympic final** at the Bird's Nest in a world record time. He also broke the world record in the 200m.

2009 Jenson Button and Brawn GP secure their first and only **F1 Drivers' Championship** and Constructors' Championship titles, respectively.
In an incident that shocked the entire sporting world, the **Sri Lankan cricket team** was attacked by terrorists while heading to the stadium to play a match.

21st Century

2010 At his debut in the US, Amir Khan, the British boxer retains his **WBA Light Welterweight** title for the second time.
Alberto Contador of Spain, wins his 3rd **Tour de France** and 5th Grand Tour.

2011 Rory McIlroy fired a 69 in the final round of the **US Open**, breaking the record with a 268 and winning by eight strokes. He becomes the youngest US Open winner since Bobby Jones in 1923.

2012 At the **London Olympics** on 'Super Saturday', Jessica Ennis-Hill, Greg Rutherford and Mo Farah all win gold in an unforgettable 44 minutes inside the Olympic Stadium. On this one single day twelve British athletes win gold medals across six events

Bradley Wiggins wins the **Tour de France**, the first British rider ever to do so and Mark Cavendish wins the final stage on the Champs-Élysées for a record fourth successive year.

2013 The **Boston Marathon** is bombed by terrorists. At **Wimbldon**, Andy Murray defeats Novak Djokovic to become the first British winner of the **Men's Singles** since Fred Perry in 1936. He earns his second Grand Slam title

2014 The first ever Invictus Games is hosted in London with over 400 competitors from 13 nations. The FA Cup Final is won by Arsenal, a joint record 11th Cup having beaten Hull City 4-3 after extra time.

2015 In Golf, Jordan Spieth led from the start in the **Masters**, shooting a record-tying 270, 18 under, to win his first major at the age of 21. Later in the year he also wins the U.S. Open.
The **Grand National** at Aintree is won by 'Many Clouds' ridden by Leighton Aspell, his second consecutive Grand National Victory.

2016 Leicester City, 5,000-1 outsiders for the title, win the **Premier League.**
Former Leicester City player Gary Lineker stated that if Leicester won the league, he would present Match of the Day in his underwear!

2017 Roger Federer becomes the undisputed **King of Wimbledon** with his record 8th win.
Chris Froome wins his 4th **Tour de France**.
In the **Women's World Cup Cricket**, England beat India by nine runs in the final at Lords.

2018 The **Tour de France** general classification was won by Geraint Thomas of Team Sky, his first win.
Roger Bannister, the first man to run a four-minute mile died this year.

2019 At the **Cheltenham Festival**, 'Frodon' ridden by Bryony Frost wins the Ryanair Chase. She is the first woman to ride a Grade One winner at Cheltenham.
Tiger Woods wins his first major in 11 years at the **Masters**.

2020 At the Tokyo Olympics, Lamont Jacobs wins the **100m** sprint and is the new **'World's Fastest Man'**.

123

Britain's Extreme

1947: Britain was struck this year by 'the perfect storm'. Record snowfall followed by a sudden thaw which culminated in heavy rain produced what is widely considered to be Britain's worst flood. Over 100,000 homes were directly affected and over 750,000 hectares of farmland submerged. The damages at the time totalled around £12 million, £300 million in today's terms.

1952: In August, the tiny village of Lynmouth, north Devon, suffered the worst river flood in English history. On the 15th, just over 9in (230mm) of rain fell over north Devon and west Somerset. The East and West Lyn rivers flooded and tons of water, soil, boulders and vegetation descended over Exmoor to meet at sea level in Lynmouth. The village was destroyed. The West Lyn rose 60 ft (18.25 m) above the normal level at its highest point and 34 people lost their lives.

1953: The great North Sea flood of January caused catastrophic damage and loss of life in Scotland, England, Belgium and The Netherlands and was Britain's worst peacetime disaster on record claiming the lives of 307 people. There were no severe flood warnings in place and the combination of gale-force winds, low pressure and high tides brought havoc to over 1,000 miles of coastline and 32,000 people were displaced because of flooding.

1963: Britain had the coldest winter in living memory, lasting for three long months from Dec 1962. The 6th March 1963 was the first morning of the year without frost anywhere in Britain.
It was so cold that rivers, lakes and even the sea froze over. On 25 February a record low of -22c in Braemar was recorded and 95,000 miles of road were snowbound.

1987: The Hurricane that wasn't supposed to be! Weatherman Michael Fish, like other forecasters, didn't see it coming. Eighteen people died and over 15 million trees were lost when in October, the hurricane-force winds blasted through south-east England. Meteorological research revealed a completely new weather phenomenon called the 'sting jet', a 100mph wind, the first to be documented in Britain.

WEATHER

2003: In August a new UK record was set for the 'Hottest Day in History' when temperatures reached 38.5c (101.3f) in Faversham, Kent. By the end of the summer, the heat had claimed the lives of over 2,000 people in Britain, mostly through heat stroke or dehydration.

An almost empty reservoir

2004: A flash flood submerged the Cornish village of Boscastle during the busy holiday period when over 60 mm of rain (typically a month's rainfall) fell in two hours. The ground was already saturated due to two weeks of above average rainfall and the Jordan and Valency rivers burst their banks causing about two billion litres of water to rush down the valley straight into Boscastle. This led to the flash flood which caused total devastation to the area, but miraculously, no loss of life.

1976: Britain had its hottest three months in living memory and it should have been the perfect summer, but with the continued sunshine came the worst drought in 150 years. Rivers dried up, soil began to crack and water supplies were on the verge of running out in Britain's most dramatic heatwave of the 20th Century. The drought was so rare, Britain appointed its first ever minister for drought, Denis Howell. He was nicknamed the minister for rain as the day after they installed him the heavens opened for the next two months!

2000: Following a wet spring and early summer, the autumn was the wettest on record for over 270 years. Repeated heavy rainfall in October and November caused significant and extensive flooding, inundated 10,000 homes and businesses. Train services cancelled, major motorways closed, and power supplies disrupted.

2007: Summer 2007 was the wettest on record with 414.1mm of rain falling across England and Wales in May, June and July - more than at any time since records began in 1766.
Although the rain was exceptionally heavy, climatologists say it was not the result of global warming. A report by the Centre for Ecology and Hydrology concluded the rain was a freak event, not part of any historical trend.

GLOBAL DISASTERS OF

Australian Bush Fires

Australia experienced the worst bushfire season ever in 2019-2020 with fires blazing for months in large parts of the country. Around 126,000 square kilometres of land and thousands of buildings were destroyed and at least 33 people died. Victoria and New South Wales were the worst affected and a state of emergency was declared in the capital city, Canberra.

Australia is used to bushfires, they are a natural part of the country's summer and native trees like eucalyptus need the heat for their seeds to be released, but this season they started earlier than usual, spread much faster, burned hotter and lasted longer, from June 2019 until March 2020, with the worst of the fires happening in December and January.

2019 was Australia's hottest and driest year on record with temperatures hitting 40c and above in every state and these hot, dry and windy conditions made the fires bigger and more intense than normal.

The Indian Ocean Tsunami

In the early morning of December 26, 2004, there was a massive and sudden movement of the Earth's crust under the Indian Ocean. This earthquake was recorded at magnitude 9 on the Richter Scale and as it happened under the ocean, the sea floor was pushed upwards, by as much as 40m, displacing a huge volume of water and causing the devastating tsunami which hit the shores of Indonesia, Sri Lanka, India, Thailand, and the Maldives.

Within 20 minutes the waves, reaching 30 feet high, and racing at the speed of a jet aircraft, engulfed the shoreline of Banda Aceh on the northern tip of Sumatra, killing more than 100,000 people and pounding the city into rubble. Then, moving on to Thailand, India and Sri Lanka, an estimated total of 250,000 people were killed, including many tourists on the beaches of Thailand. Millions more people were displaced, and eight hours later, and 5,000 miles from its Asian epicentre, the tsunami claimed its final casualties on the coast of South Africa.

The 21st Century

Hurricane Katrina

Hurricane Katrina hit the coast of Louisiana on 29th August 2005. A Category 3 storm, it caused destruction from central Florida to Texas, but most lives were lost, and damage caused in New Orleans. It passed over Miami where the 80mph winds uprooted trees and killed two people. Hurricanes need warm ocean water to keep up speed and strength, so Katrina weakened whilst over the land to a tropical storm. Crossing back into the Gulf of Mexico, it quickly regained hurricane status and at its largest, was so wide, its diameter stretched right across the Gulf. Katrina crossed back over the coast near Biloxi, Mississippi, where winds were the strongest and damage was extensive. However, later that morning, the first of 50 old levees broke in New Orleans, and a surge of floodwater poured into the low-lying city.

COVID 19 A Global Pandemic

The first human cases of COVID-19, the coronavirus disease caused by SARS CoV-2, were first reported from Wuhan City, China, in December 2019. Environmental samples taken in a food market in Wuhan where wild and farmed animals were traded, were positive for the virus and it is still unconfirmed whether the market was the origin of the virus or was just the setting for its initial spread.

The virus spread rapidly throughout China and has been found in 202 other countries, reaching Britain, from Europe, in late January 2020 and in March, the 'Stay at Home Order' or lockdown, was introduced. Non-essential travel was banned, schools were shut along with many businesses and venues. We were told to stay 6ft apart from others, self-isolate and, if at risk, to shield.

How Attitudes Have Changed

Sex and Sexism Sells

Attitudes towards many aspects of our lives have changed significantly since the 1970s. One very entertaining way to see some of these changes is to look at the advertisements of the times.

Smirnoff made fun of the feminism movement in the 1970s.

TOWARDS WOMEN

1971: Change was about to happen, 'Because I'm Worth It' reflected women's rights, encouraging women to embrace their ambitions fearlessly and believe in their self-worth every day.

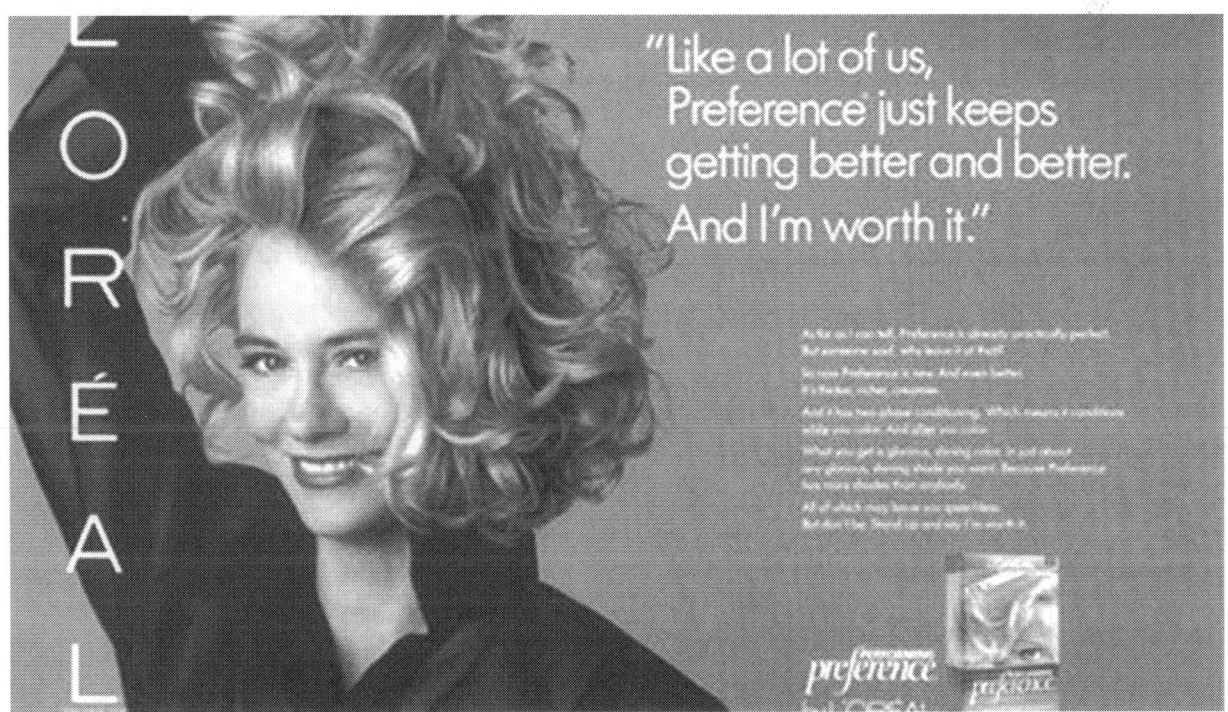

There can still be subtle sexism in adverts today. Research is showing that when people are portrayed in general, not just men or women, in non-stereotypical ways the ads perform better.

How Attitudes Have Changed

Size Matters

In Great Britain, cars were smaller in the 70s than they are now. A four-seater, just big enough for you, the family and a couple of suitcases was the norm, you didn't have to squeeze into parking spaces and there was no need to dread driving down country lanes. By the 21st Century, cars have become bigger and the ubiquitous SUV is everywhere. Even the not-so Mini Cooper has evolved since lorry drivers struggled to see the car in their side view mirrors and is now 61% bigger than the original.

The major reasons for the increase in size are firstly, they are produced abroad and therefore not designed with the British roads in mind; safety considerations such as airbags and crumple zones need more room to accommodate; manufacturers can charge more for a larger car whilst the cost of producing it is not much more than producing a small car and finance deals have removed the necessity of finding the cash up front and enable the purchase of bigger, luxury, models.

THE MINI THEN
Length 120ins Width 50ins Weight 580Kg

THE MINI 60 YEARS LATER
Length 150ins Width 68ins Weight 1150Kg

THE FORD FIESTA THEN
Length 140ins Width 62ins Weight 750Kg

THE FORD FIESTA 60 YEARS LATER
Length 160ins Width 69ins Weight 1200Kg

In just 50 years cars have become longer, wider and much heavier. The Mini has doubled in weight, the Fiesta is 60% heavier and SUV versions of a car are wider and heavier than their saloon counterparts. SUVs are very popular but use more fuel and have more emissions than the non SUV versions.

SUV electric cars use more electricity than non SUVs, and are more expensive to buy.

Towards Cars

THE BMW 3 SERIES THEN
Length 171ins Width 63ins Weight 1100Kg

THE BMW 3 SERIES SUV 60 YEARS LATER
Length 185ins Width 74ins Weight 1885Kg

THE ROLLS ROYCE CULLIAN OF 2023
Length 210ins Width 80ins Weight 2739Kg

How In Car Technology Has Changed

The 70s introduced the in-car cassette tape player

The 80s brought the CD-Radio player

The 90s brought in car telephones

The 2020s brought in self driving cars

And the future? Manufacturers are already working on making displays that respond to gestures, no touch screens necessary; you will be able to start your car or open the boot with your fingerprint and all the information you might need will be displayed on 'smart glass' in your windscreen!

How Attitudes Have Changed

It is a truth now universally acknowledged that smoking is bad for your health, but it wasn't always so. Cigarettes had been promoted as 'healthy', socially improving and fun! Some brands kept customer loyalty by offering gift vouchers.

As early as 1950 a report in the British Medical Journal had suggested a link between smoking and lung cancer and by 1962 the Royal College of Physicians had enough evidence to push for a ban on advertising.

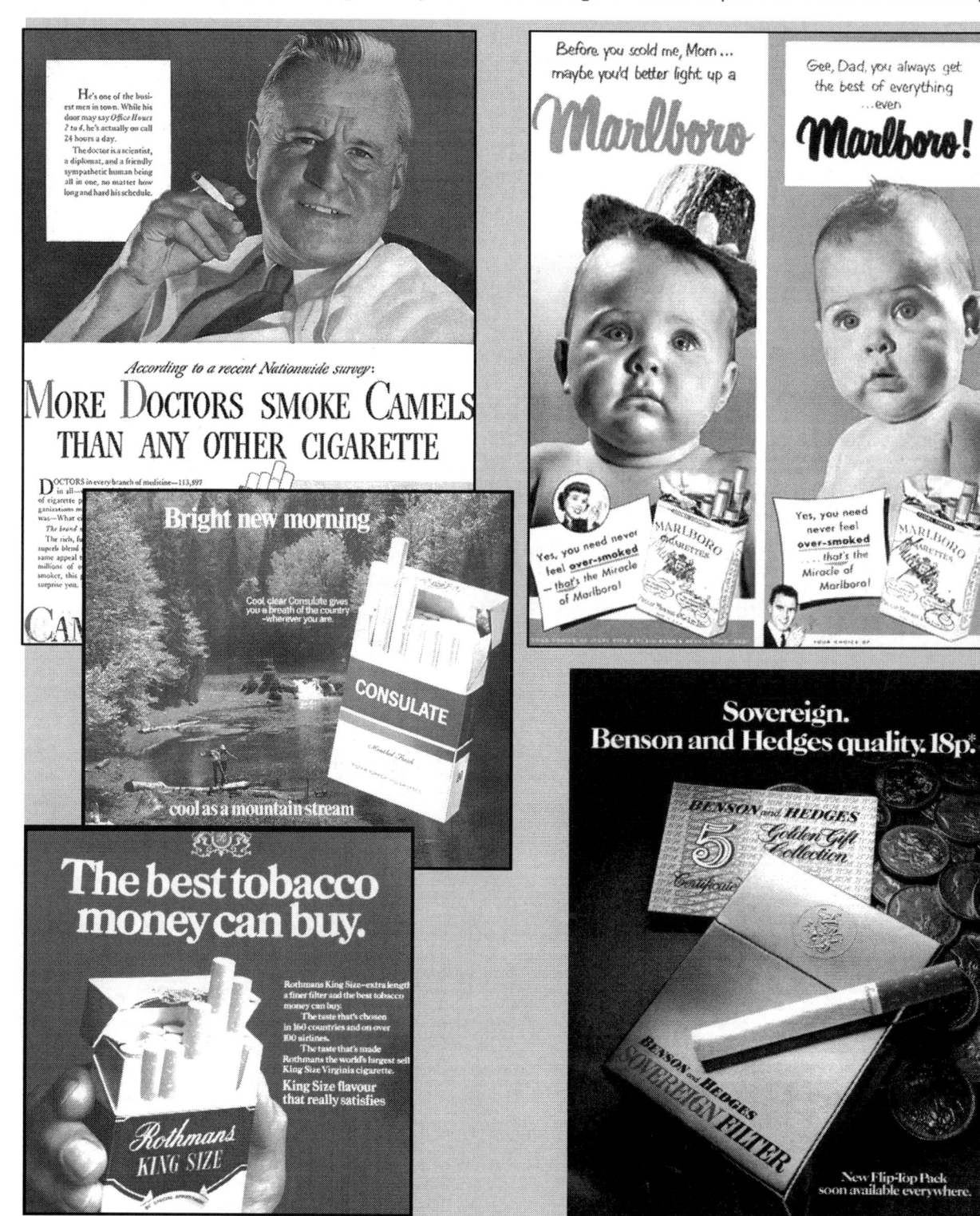

Towards Smoking

Time Line of Law Changes

1965: Television Commercials Banned

1971: All cigarette packets required a warning stating "WARNING by H.M. Government, SMOKING CAN DAMAGE YOUR HEALTH".

1982: The British Medical Association requested a ban on all forms of tobacco advertising.

1986: In 1986 adverts were banned in cinemas and it wasn't permitted to show a person smoking in an ad for any product or service.

1987: Smoking and cigarette advertising is banned on the underground – but more for safety reasons than those of health.

1991: The EU stated that all cigarettes must have two warnings on the packet, one on the front stating 'TOBACCO SERIOUSLY DAMAGES HEALTH' and another warning on the back such as "Smoking clogs the arteries and causes heart attacks and strokes".

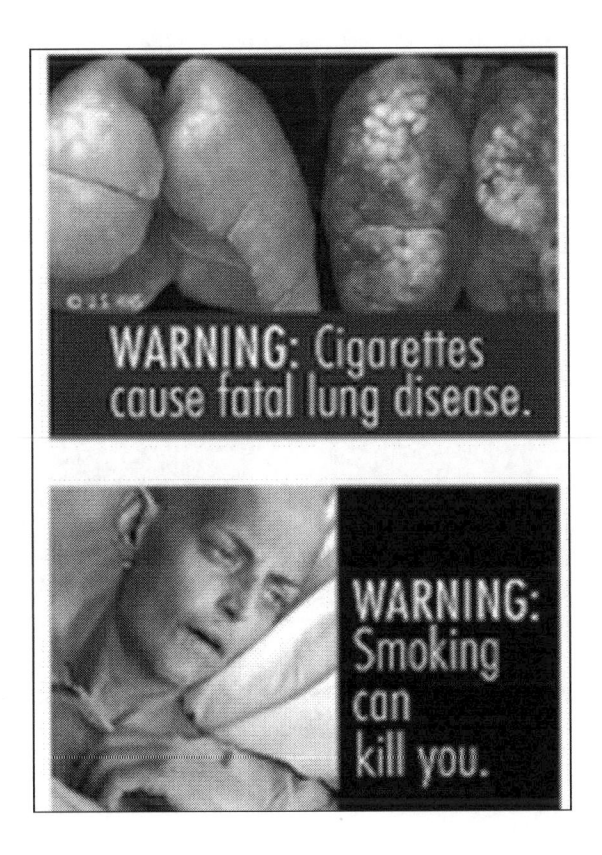

2002: The Tobacco Advertising and Promotion Act aims to wipe out tobacco advertising by 2005, including general advertising, promotions, sponsored events in the UK and sponsorship of global events including Formula 1 and snooker tournaments.

2003: Further EU sanctions made it illegal to brand cigarettes as 'mild' or 'light', and warnings on cigarette packets are enlarged; one covering at least 30% of the packet has to state either 'Smoking Kills' or 'Smoking seriously harms you and others around you'.

2003: The British government invest £31 million in *anti*-smoking campaigns.

2007: It becomes illegal to smoke in public places in the UK such as bars, restaurants and shopping centres and the legal age limit for purchasing tobacco was raised by two years to 18, however the minimum age for possession remained 16

How Attitudes Have Changed

Exercise as a leisure activity was not invented in the last 50 years but the global focus on fitness has undeniably increased. Having a treadmill in your house in 1970 would have been unusual but now it's normal to have equipment at home as well as membership of a local gym or health centre. Both sexes are now expected to keep themselves in shape.

1970s: Fitness, as we know it today, seemed to start with the running boom of the 1970s, primarily a 'jogging' movement in which running was generally pursued alone for recreation and fitness but also a growth in competitive running events in public.

With the advent of the "fun run" the general public suddenly perked up to the joys of running.

Brands like Adidas, Puma, and Nike dominated the running shoe, trainers, market, but every company heard the call for performance-enhancing running shoes. Nike's use of innovative designs and materials ultimately ushered in the arrival of modern-day running shoes.

In the 1970s, workouts were monotonous exercise routines. But all that changed with the advent of the Jazzercise craze. In 1969, dance instructor Judi Sheppard Missett created a dynamic new exercise blending dance, kickboxing, Pilates and yoga. This combination of aerobic exercise and jazz dancing was designed to slim and tone.

Towards Health & Fitness

1980s: High energy aerobic workouts became the fashion and the meteoric rise of home workout videos, led by Jane Fonda, spurred on the popularity of step aerobics. The trend saw millions of people spending good money on small plastic blocks to step on and off repeatedly.

1990s: Mr Motivator, the Jamaican-born British fitness instructor rose to fame through appearances on the UK breakfast television where he performed live fitness sessions and offered tips and advice to viewers. In America, Billy Blanks, a taekwondo instructor, brought Tae Bo to the nation with a combination of taekwondo and boxing.

Roller blading (in line skates) took the place of the 1970s roller skates. There were plenty of gimmicks too. The Shake Weight, a dumbbell with springs attached to the weights, that oscillates in your hand when you jiggle it, alleged to work your upper body more efficiently than a standard dumbbell.

2000s: the decade in which fitness through dance returned. 'Street dance' passed through school yards and local neighbourhoods into dance studios and gyms.

2010: Fast paced Zumba arrived, incorporating elements of hip-hop, salsa, samba, meringue and mambo. Classes, videos and Nintendo games all fuelled the craze. HIIT workouts 'hit' the spot! We've come a long way since the Hula Hoop!

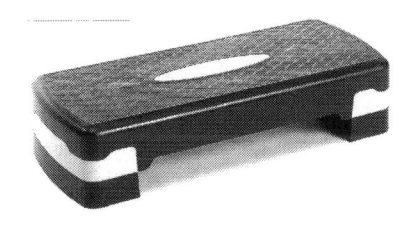

How Attitudes Have Changed

From Corner Shop to Supermarket

There have been major changes to the British diet since the 1970s and by the 21st century, the story of the modern British dinner table is less home cooking, more prepared and takeaway meals; less fish and chips and vastly more meals reflecting our changing culture - more Italian, Indian, SE Asian and North American 'fast food'.

We shop differently. In the 1970s we bought meat at the butcher, fish at the fishmonger, fruit and vegetables at the greengrocer but now 85% of our grocery shopping is at the supermarket and 14% of that is on line. Supermarkets carry a huge range of products including previously unknown salad leaves, spices, exotic fruit and vegetables.

The move towards ever faster food continued. In 1980, the average meal took one hour to prepare. By 1999, that had dropped to 20 minutes. This change was driven by the increasing number of working women and the availability of ready meals. Between 1974 and 2014 "ready meals and convenience meat products" went up five fold.

More people were living on their own, further fuelling the market for fast food. This is matched by a drop in the popularity of fresh, canned and tinned food. The amount of canned peas bought dropped by two thirds between 1974 and 2014. Purchases of white bread have dropped 75% while those of brown and wholemeal bread have risen by 85%. Consumption of eggs peaked in the 1960s and has been declining ever since. Bananas replaced apples as the most popular fruit in 1996. There has been a 30% reduction in fresh vegetables and fruit, we buy many fewer carrots, turnips, parsnips, cabbages and sprouts.

Offal has fallen out of favour among younger, more squeamish Britons. In 1974 a typical household bought 36g of liver per week, but by 2014 the figure had fallen to just 3g - a 92% drop. Pork and mutton also saw more modest falls in popularity, while consumption of uncooked chicken and minced beef rose 62% and 35% over the same period respectively.

Towards Our Food

Burgers, Chips and Pizza

Dried and fresh pasta was not even recorded on the National Food Survey until 1998. Between then and 2014, weekly household purchases in this category more than doubled. Pizza rose even more dramatically, with an average purchase from 2g per week in 1975 to 53g in 2014.

The number of takeaway pizzas bought per household shot up 1,000% over the same period. Burgers came to Britain in the 1970s and we eat 2.5 billion beef burgers a year. That roughly works out at the average Brit eating 37 burgers annually. A study of 2,000 adults also found 83% of those who eat meat and fish couldn't 'live' without them.

The nation still loves chips. Sales were three times higher in 2014 than in 1974. However, households reported buying a third less takeaway chips over the same period and the traditional accompaniment has fared differently. In 1974 we bought 44g of white fish - fresh, chilled or frozen - per week and while it is still the most popular fish choice, we buy just 19g a week.

Other types of seafood has done better. Shellfish purchases rose five fold, and those of salmon by 550%.

Consumption of the UK's preferred hot drink, tea, has declined steadily since 1974, from 68g per week to 25g. However, tea remains more popular than instant coffee, cocoa and malted drinks, and the decline has been attributed to "the coffee culture in the UK" and the decline in popularity of sweet biscuits! We drink 12 times as much bottled water now as we did in the 1980s. Skimmed and semi-skimmed milk overtook whole-fat milk in the 1990s and British households now drink four times as much.

How Attitudes Have Changed

More is Better

'More was certainly better' in the decades following the war and particularly for children. School meals were a way of providing a hot, nutritious meal for every child and free school milk was given out every day to provide all important calcium. In the 1970s, school dinners were 'balanced', typically meat or fish and two veg. Fish and chips with peas or liver and mash with greens, followed by jam roly-poly with custard or rice pudding. Yet this new prosperity was something of a poisoned chalice in relation to the health of the population, obesity was first recognised as a 'hazard to health' in the UK in 1976. Things became worse in 1980 when The Education Act abolished the minimum nutritional standards for school meals and removed the statutory obligation to provide meals for all children.

A 1970s school meal - main course

The introduction of commercial tendering for school meals resulted in private companies bringing in 'a free-choice, cafeteria system'. The result - the easy option of burgers, chips and chocolate cake. Our children were being fed high calorie, junk food.

A 1990s school meal of Turkey Twizzlers, Smiley potato and beans with a sweet dessert

By the 2000s there was a push towards healthier food in schools and turkey twizzlers disappeared from the school canteen, being replaced with options such as fish curry, bean wraps, pasta dishes and salads. However, the trend was still for more and faster food, snacking continued to rise and the intake of fruit and vegetables declined.

A modern day school meal of lasagna, vegetables with fruit and yogurt.

Towards Nutrition

Too Much Can Be Bad

As the 21st Century unravels before us, obesity levels are on a meteoric rise. The most obvious explanation for this is that we are a lot less active now than we were in the 70s. We walk a lot less and do less physical work. We snack more and consume a growing number of calories from sugary drinks, crisps and chocolate. We eat more processed foods and ready meals which are still high in sugar and salt. Computers, diet, TV and an 80% reduction in exercise at school, as it no longer holds the importance in the children's week, has contributed to childhood obesity. In the 2010s, the rise of the smartphone had a huge impact on our eating and health habits. Fast food delivery became available literally at our fingertips and online streaming meant we could spend hours on the sofa bingeing on our favourite television shows. During the Covid 19 'lock downs', whilst gyms closed and people worked from home, ordering fast food or cooking lavishly at home became one of the few remaining pleasures to enjoy.

However, we *are* more aware of the issue of obesity and unhealthy lifestyles. Foods carry nutritional information on their packages, salt and sugar content has been reduced in processed food and thanks to public opinion, McDonalds provide salads, 'bottomless' fizzy drinks are no longer the norm and restaurants are obliged to add a calorie count to their menus

Crispy Chicken Salad
1092 kJ | 261 kcal
Freshly prepared salad with chicken breast in a crispy coating, lettuce, cucumber, sliced tomato

BURGERS

Hamburger
255 Calories
10g Fat
29g Carbs
13g Protein

Cheeseburger
300 Calories
13g Fat
30g Carbs
15g Protein

Double Cheeseburger
410 Calories
21g Fat
30g Carbs
24g Protein

Bacon Cheeseburger
340 Calories
16g Fat
30g Carbs
18g Protein

Bacon Double Cheeseburger
450 Calories
25g Fat
31g Carbs
27g Protein

Whopper Jr.
335 Calories
19g Fat
30g Carbs
15g Protein

The best news is, our average life expectancy is much better than it was. In 1970, the average person was expected to live to 72, while today that has increased to 81.

How Attitudes Have Changed

HOME WORKING

50 years ago, "going to work" meant heading to a physical location outside of your home and working there until 5pm. Today, your spare bedroom or dining room is just as likely to be your office. 43% of workplaces allow employees to work from home at least part of the time. If you DO go to the office, rather than wearing a suit or dress, you are more likely to be wearing jeans and trainers!

COMMUNICATIONS

Back in the 1970s, if you wanted to get in touch – faster than writing a letter and posting it - with a friend, you rang them up on a land-line phone and asked how they were doing. Now, we can see what our friends are up to on their social media. How their relationships are going, where they go on holiday, and, in some cases, what they had for breakfast. Information that used to take time to convey, is now delivered in a second by text or app.

24 HOUR NEWS

Half a century ago, if you wanted to find out what was happening in the world, you'd have to wait for the morning paper to come out. Now the news is on television, websites and apps 24 hours a day. There are hundreds of television channels now, all running day and night. In the 70s the three channels, BBC1, BBC2 and ITV played the National Anthem at midnight and stopped broadcasting. The screens were blank until about six in the morning and of course, no 'catch up' or 'streaming' or 'television whilst you are on the go."

Towards Getting Things Done

INTERNET SHOPPING

No need now to go to the shop anymore, clothes, music, groceries – anything you can think of – is brought to you with a tap on your computer, tablet or smartphone.

MEETING AND DATING

Dating 50 years ago meant one of two things. You met someone you liked out in the world and exchanged numbers, or you had someone set you up.

Today, hundreds of potential partners are just a swipe away, thanks to the proliferation of dating apps. Marriage is no longer expected, families are smaller and getting older goes on for longer!

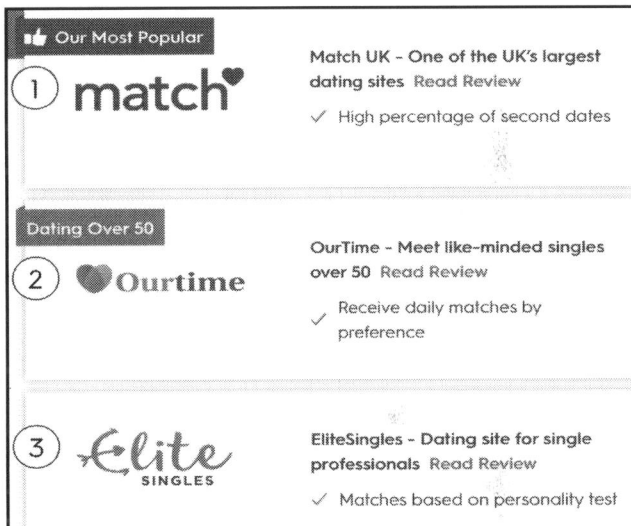

LEISURE

Board games, cards and dominoes have given way to computer games and virtual reality promises travel and other experiences without leaving your sofa! Everyone can watch whatever they want wherever they want on a phone, tablet or computer. You meet and speak with family and friends more via an app than by face to face. We watch more sport, but play less.

1964 Calendar

	January					
S	M	T	W	T	F	S
			1	2	3	4
5	6	7	8	9	10	11
12	13	14	15	16	17	18
19	20	21	22	23	24	25
26	27	28	29	30	31	

	February					
S	M	T	W	T	F	S
						1
2	3	4	5	6	7	8
9	10	11	12	13	14	15
16	17	18	19	20	21	22
23	24	25	26	27	28	29

	March					
S	M	T	W	T	F	S
1	2	3	4	5	6	7
8	9	10	11	12	13	14
15	16	17	18	19	20	21
22	23	24	25	26	27	28
29	30	31				

	April					
S	M	T	W	T	F	S
			1	2	3	4
5	6	7	8	9	10	11
12	13	14	15	16	17	18
19	20	21	22	23	24	25
26	27	28	29	30		

	May					
S	M	T	W	T	F	S
					1	2
3	4	5	6	7	8	9
10	11	12	13	14	15	16
17	18	19	20	21	22	23
24	25	26	27	28	29	30
31						

	June					
S	M	T	W	T	F	S
	1	2	3	4	5	6
7	8	9	10	11	12	13
14	15	16	17	18	19	20
21	22	23	24	25	26	27
28	29	30				

	July					
S	M	T	W	T	F	S
			1	2	3	4
5	6	7	8	9	10	11
12	13	14	15	16	17	18
19	20	21	22	23	24	25
26	27	28	29	30	31	

	August					
S	M	T	W	T	F	S
						1
2	3	4	5	6	7	8
9	10	11	12	13	14	15
16	17	18	19	20	21	22
23	24	25	26	27	28	29
30	31					

	September					
S	M	T	W	T	F	S
		1	2	3	4	5
6	7	8	9	10	11	12
13	14	15	16	17	18	19
20	21	22	23	24	25	26
27	28	29	30			

	October					
S	M	T	W	T	F	S
				1	2	3
4	5	6	7	8	9	10
11	12	13	14	15	16	17
18	19	20	21	22	23	24
25	26	27	28	29	30	31

	November					
S	M	T	W	T	F	S
1	2	3	4	5	6	7
8	9	10	11	12	13	14
15	16	17	18	19	20	21
22	23	24	25	26	27	28
29	30					

	December					
S	M	T	W	T	F	S
		1	2	3	4	5
6	7	8	9	10	11	12
13	14	15	16	17	18	19
20	21	22	23	24	25	26
27	28	29	30	31		

Printed in Great Britain
by Amazon

20fae5dd-2ed2-4db2-9246-7404da6ceda2R01